# POLITICAL AND SOCIAL ISSUES IN CHRISTIAN-MUSLIM RELATIONS TODAY:

## THE QUESTIONS CHRISTIANS ASK

**Second edition**

by

Peter G Riddell

The Arthur Jeffery Centre for the Study of Islam
Melbourne School of Theology
2017

ISBN 978-0-9876154-4-2
© 2017 Melbourne School of Theology Press. All rights reserved.


**Production and Cover Design**
Ho-yuin Chan


**Publishing Services**
Published by Melbourne School of Theology Press

**The Arthur Jeffery Centre for the Study of Islam**
Melbourne School of Theology
5 Burwood Highway, Wantirna, Victoria 3152, Australia.
PO Box 6257, Vermont Sth, Victoria 3133, Australia
Ph: +61 3 9881 7800, Fax: +61 3 9800 0121
info@jefferycentre.mst.edu.au, www.mst.edu.au

This is a revised edition of chapter 6 of
Peter G. Riddell, *Christians and Muslims: pressures and potential in a post-9/11 world* (Leicester: Inter-Varsity Press, 2004), based on the London Lectures in Contemporary Christianity, 2003.

**PREFACE** ............................................................................................. 7

**INTRODUCTION** ............................................................................... 9
   Christian – Muslim stereotypes about each other ............................. 9
   The transmission of stereotypes ....................................................... 11
   From the centre to the periphery ...................................................... 13
   Greater Christian awareness ............................................................ 16
   Conclusion ....................................................................................... 20

**MUSLIM PLURALITY** ..................................................................... 21
   Does Islam have denominations like Christianity? .......................... 21
   Are there serious dialogues between radical Muslims and other Muslims? ........................................................................................... 22
   Should Christians make a decision as to who are real Muslims? ...... 23
   So what is Islam? ............................................................................. 24

**CHRISTIAN PLURALITY** ................................................................ 27
   Do Christian denominational divisions provide fuel for some Muslims who seek to discredit Christians and their faith? ............................. 27
   What is the general Christian perception of Islam and vice-versa? ... 27

**INTERNATIONAL CRISES** .............................................................. 31
   How central is the Israel issue to Christian-Muslim relations around the world? ........................................................................................ 31
   So is the conflict surrounding the state of Israel a root cause of Islamic radicalism? .......................................................................... 32
   How should Christians respond to the international political crises of the early 21$^{st}$ century? ................................................................. 33
   Is Christianity more supportive of globalisation, industrialisation, and capitalism than Islam? ............................................................... 36
   Is a clash between the West and Islam inevitable? ........................... 36
   Do Muslims welcome non-Muslim campaigns against terrorism? ... 37
   Is there a link between terrorism and refugees? ............................... 39

**HUMAN RIGHTS UNDER ISLAM** .................................................. 41
   Teachings in Islamic Scripture ......................................................... 43
   Application in the modern world ..................................................... 44
   Dissenting Muslims voices .............................................................. 46
   How should Christians respond? ..................................................... 46
   What about the anti-reciprocity argument? ...................................... 47

**RELIGION, SOCIETY AND THE PUBLIC DISCOURSE** ............... 51
   Is religion now back on the public agenda in the West? .................. 51

How should Christians respond to the push for Shariah Law in Western countries? ................................................................. 52
How should Christians respond to a mosque being built in their neighbourhood? .................................................................... 54
Is the term "multi-faith" appropriate for Western countries? ......... 57
Should Christians embrace the People of Faith notion? .................. 58
What is the future of multi-faith Western societies? ..................... 61

## WHERE DOES SPIRITUAL WARFARE COME INTO CHRISTIAN-MUSLIM RELATIONS? .................................................................................... 65
The too-liberal approach ................................................................ 65
The too-literal approach ................................................................ 66
Reflections ..................................................................................... 66

## EVALUATING ISLAM ........................................................................ 69
Is Islam a religion of peace? ........................................................... 69
Is terrorism more likely to flow out of Islam than Christianity? ...... 71
How should Islam be studied? ........................................................ 72
If we'd like to understand Islam more should we read the Qur'an for ourselves? ....................................................................................... 74
Muslims criticise the Bible and say that it is not reliable and accurate. How reliable and accurate is the Qur'an? ....................................... 74

## TRUTH AND CHRISTIAN-MUSLIM RELATIONS ................................. 77
How do we deal with conflicting truth claims? .............................. 80
Perennial truths and the place of Jesus ......................................... 80

## CHRISTIAN APPROACHES TO ISLAM ............................................... 83
Is there a more helpful mindset to approaching Muslims than just "Conversion"? ................................................................................. 83
What are the objectives of inter-faith dialogue? ............................ 83
What are the best ways to do interfaith dialogue? ........................ 86
Are there any prerequisites for interfaith dialogue? ...................... 87
Who should Christians be dialoguing with? ................................... 88
Which Muslims should Christians be talking to? ............................ 90
Why do Christians lack confidence and how can they best deal with it? .................................................................................................... 90
Should Christians pray with people from other faiths? .................. 91
How can Christians minister to Muslim women without causing family chaos? ................................................................................ 91
Should Christians watch their language? ....................................... 91

> DO CHRISTIANS HAVE THE RIGHT TO ASK CRITICAL QUESTIONS ABOUT CORE ISLAMIC BELIEFS?....................................................................... 94
> WHAT IS THE ATTITUDE OF THE ORTHODOX CHURCHES IN RELATION TO DIALOGUE WITH ISLAM? ........................................................ 97
> HOW SHOULD CHRISTIANS AND MUSLIMS REPORT PAST HISTORY? ............. 100

**FURTHER QUESTIONS....................................................................103**
> QUESTIONS ABOUT THEOLOGY AND EVANGELISM ..................................... 103
> QUESTIONS TO ASK MUSLIMS WHEN VISITING A MOSQUE.......................... 104

**BIBLIOGRAPHY..............................................................................109**

# Preface

The first edition of this work appeared as Chapter 6 in my book, *Christians and Muslims: Pressures and potential in a post-9/11 world* (Leicester: Inter-Varsity Press, 2004).[1] That volume represented the published version of the London Lectures in Contemporary Christianity for 2003, for which the late Rev Dr John Stott was Patron and which I delivered at the London Institute for Contemporary Christianity.

The period of those 2003 lectures was especially dynamic in terms of Christian-Muslim relations, coming in the wake of the Al-Qaeda terrorist attacks on the World Trade Centre in New York and the Pentagon on September 11, 2001. The audiences for the 2003 lectures were particularly interested to pose questions on political and social issues as they relate to Christian-Muslim relations.

The 9/11 terrorist attacks did not represent the beginning of the current wave of Islamic resurgence. In fact, the dynamic resurgence of Islamic identity that we are witnessing today has been underway across the world since the 1970s. This has been fuelled by rapidly increasing revenue for the Islamic world from oil income, and new or resurrected expressions of Islam have come to the fore. On the one hand, some Muslims have pushed at the boundaries of liberal thinking, seeking to bring the world of Islam into the era of human rights, the digital age and cyberspace. At the same time, rapid progress has produced a throwback mentality among some Muslims, expressed in threatening terms by fundamentalist movements, including radical groups such as the notorious Al-Qaeda, the Islamic State in Iraq and Syria and the lesser known Hizbut Tahrir.

At the same time, dramatic movements of Muslim populations have led to the rise of significant Muslim minority communities hosting these various expressions of Islamic faith in Western countries. In Britain, for example, the Muslim community has grown from around 400,000 in the mid-1970s to well over 3,000,000 today. Australia has seen its Muslim minority grow during the same period from barely 20,000 to over 600,000. Similar growth has taken place in other Western countries.

---

[1] That book, less its sixth chapter, is currently being revised as a second edition.

Since the 2003 London Lectures, I have continued to speak on Islam and Christian-Muslim Relations in churches and other venues in Britain, Australia, New Zealand, the USA, France, and Malaysia. It has been noticeable that similar questions arise again and again in these diverse locations about wide-ranging methods of interaction between Christians and Muslims, be they evangelistic, social, political, and other styles of engagement. The audiences in these events have been mostly Christian, whether practicing or nominal.

This present volume represents a collection of those questions and my answers during and since the 2003 London Lectures. I have deliberately chosen to focus on questions that relate to politics and society, rather than questions that relate to evangelistic method, which are well treated in works by other authors. I have grouped the questions according to a set of themes and have tried to keep the discussion non-specialised and accessible to as wide a Christian readership as possible.

Of course, a different set of questions might be asked by Muslims to Christians, or indeed, by Christians to Muslims. On many occasions, I have taken classes that I have taught in various theological institutions to mosques. A selection of questions prepared by my students in such interactions is provided in an appendix, though I have not attempted to reproduce answers to those questions in this volume.

It is hoped that this volume will prove helpful to Christians who would like to ask these questions but do not have the opportunity to attend events where they are discussed. I am indebted to all who have attended my public talks over the years and who have posed these and other questions in those events.

Peter Riddell
Melbourne, September 2017

## Introduction[2]

Spokespeople for Islam often express the view that the religion is the victim of negative media portrayals in the West, leading to misunderstanding by non-Muslims of the true nature of Islam. The following quote from a book by the author Louay Fatoohi expresses this well:

> "Islam has been the subject of a great deal of misunderstanding and misrepresentation. It is not uncommon to see this religion being portrayed in the media, explicitly and implicitly, as an enemy of modern good values such as democracy, liberty, and tolerance."[3]

This claim has weighed heavily on my mind over the years. A key part of the reason is that I have been giving public lectures and teaching tertiary courses on Islam since the mid 1990s. In that time, I have been asked a myriad of questions by mainly Christian audiences about a range of issues, covering theology, history, politics and society. I have always had difficulty matching my perception of the relatively well-informed nature of my audiences with the claim that Western audiences are fed a continuous stream of false information about Islam.

To enable a closer examination of this charge, I have assembled a wide range of questions that have been posed by Christian audiences in my public lectures over the years. I will make an assessment as to whether these questions reflect widespread ignorance or rather a good basis of knowledge among those audiences. But before we proceed to that primary task, it would be helpful to reflect on the past history of Christian-Muslim perceptions of each other.

### Christian – Muslim stereotypes about each other

If we survey the tangled web of Christian-Muslim relations in today's world, we are struck by some remarkable paradoxes. On the one hand, at the level of the ordinary people, we can encounter some inspiring and heart-warming stories of Christian-Muslim cooperation and friendship. If only all Christian-Muslim interaction were of this

---

[2] The text in this introduction was given as a public lecture at Laidlaw College, Auckland, New Zealand, on 23 August 2017.

[3] Louay Fatoohi, *Jihad in the Qur'an: The Truth from the Source* (Luna Plena Publishing, 2009).

kind, it would barely be newsworthy, and that would probably be a good thing.

But only a determined ostrich would pretend that there wasn't a lot more to Christian-Muslim interaction, especially down the ages. In fact, conflict rather than cooperation between Christians and Muslims was so pervasive that particular episodes of military confrontation seem to merge together, as in accounts and paintings of cities under siege. Graphic accounts of such events could equally apply to Jerusalem under siege by the Crusaders in 1099 or Constantinople under siege by the Muslim Ottoman Turks in 1453.

One thing is clear. Stories of friendship and opposition today should not be analysed in a vacuum. Today's stories, whether positive or negative, are merely the latest layer in a multi-layered relationship going back 1400 years. It is a relationship which was at times fraught and tragic, yet with periodic episodes of renewal and more positive engagement.

Any assessment of the history of Christian-Muslim interaction must take account of the Christian-Muslim Relations Bibliographical Project that has been underway since 2008.[4] Funded by the British government, managed by the University of Birmingham and published by Brill publishers of Leiden, this project sets out to amass a comprehensive set of documents where Christians and Muslims write about, against or for each other. In other words, the multi-volume Encyclopaedia will provide a comprehensive testimony of Christian-Muslim interaction from the beginning of the 7th century to the outbreak of the First World War.

In effect, this project seeks to identify the chain of history, that phenomenon whereby a historical episode is linked in some way to what went before and what came after. This is essential in understanding Christian-Relations today, because the shared joys and bitter divisions which characterise today's situation have deep roots in the past.

We will now go on a brief journey into the distant and not so distant past, to identify how Christians and Muslims have viewed each other, starting with the foundational texts which shaped attitudes

---

[4] "The Christian-Muslim Relations projects", accessed 24 August 2017,
http://www.birmingham.ac.uk/schools/ptr/departments/theologyandreligion/research/projects/CMR1900/index.aspx.

towards the other. We will then return to consider Christian questions and perceptions today.

## The transmission of stereotypes

The Bible does not make any reference to the religion of Islam because the latest parts of the Biblical record predate the life of Muhammed by hundreds of years. Therefore, fortunately we cannot find any evidence of an overt anti-Muslim slur in the pages of either the Old Testament or the New Testament.

In the case of the Islamic primary texts, namely Qur'an and Hadith, there are many references to Jews and Christians, reflecting the fact that Muhammad interacted with both these communities in different ways in the Arabian Peninsula during his lifetime. The portrayal of Jews and Christians, while not monolithic, tends to be more negative than positive, especially for Jews. Consider the following two verses from chapter 5, which dates from a late period of Muhammad's life:

> Q5:51 *You who believe, do not take the Jews and Christians as allies: they are allies only to each other. Anyone who takes them as an ally becomes one of them — God does not guide such wrongdoers.*

> Q5:82 *You [Prophet] are sure to find that the most hostile to the believers are the Jews and those who associate other deities with God; you are sure to find that the closest in affection towards the believers are those who say, 'We are Christians,' for there are among them people devoted to learning and ascetics.*

Some Hadith accounts sow seeds of religious opposition very clearly, such as the following report given of Muhammad's final words:

> Narrated 'Aisha and 'Abdullah bin 'Abbas: *When the last moment of the life of Allah's Apostle came he started putting his 'Khamisa' on his face and when he felt hot and short of breath he took it off his face and said, "May Allah curse the Jews and Christians for they built the places of worship at the graves of their Prophets." The Prophet was warning (Muslims) of what those had done.*[5]

Here we are talking about texts, not the people who use them. And while it would be unlikely that the majority of Muslims would **consciously** draw on the texts to shape their opinions about Jews and Christians, at the same time the process of educational formation during childhood that many Muslims go through in which they study

---

[5] Bukhari, vol. 1, book 8, no 427.

such verses must necessarily sow seeds of negativity towards non-Muslims which can grow into full-blown hostility with some Muslims.

Apart from the influence of textual materials, repeated negative interactions throughout history compound inter-religious problems. The Christian and Muslim worlds were at war for much of the last 1400 years, and this continuous opposition shaped attitudes which come through in writing by followers of both faiths.

> *Typically the written records tend to capture the detail of conflict rather than cooperation, of fighting rather than friendship.*

Consider the famous Song of Roland, a late 12th century French work which lamented the defeat of the French leader Charlemagne in the Iberian Peninsula hundreds of years before. It portrays him as the victim of devious betrayal, with the Islamic religion of his opponents being presented as a pagan idolatry centred around a demonic Trinity of figures.[6]

Meanwhile, Muslim writers were producing similarly vitriolic material regarding Christians and Christianity. In a letter to the Turkish Seljuk Sultan Kayka'us in the early 13th century, the famous Andalusian Muslim mystic Ibn Arabi declared:

> "I tell you that among the worst things that can befall Islam and Muslims – and how few they are – are the ringing out of church bells, the public display of unbelief and the elevation of words of *shirk* (worship of other than God)."[7]

He supports this view with a Hadith report which states that "No church should be built in Islam, nor those of them which have fallen into ruin be restored."[8]

---

[6] "The Song of Roland", trans. John O'Hagan, accessed 25 August 2017, https://sourcebooks.fordham.edu/basis/roland-ohag.asp.

[7] Hirtenstein, Stephen, "Ibn ʿArabī", in: *Christian-Muslim Relations 600 - 1500*, General Editor David Thomas. Consulted online on 21 September 2017 <http://dx.doi.org/10.1163/1877-8054_cmri_COM_24834>. First published online: 2010

[8] Consistent with a Hadith account in *Sahih Muslim*, Book #019, Hadith #4366, which reports Muhammad saying: "I will expel the Jews and Christians from the Arabian Peninsula and will not leave any but Muslim."

One of the frustrating challenges of tracking Christian-Muslim relations down the centuries is that typically the written records tend to capture the detail of conflict rather than cooperation, of fighting rather than friendship. No doubt there were countless instances of ordinary Christians and ordinary Muslims who lived side-by-side and enjoyed cordial relationships and friendships, but the "little" people involved did not usually leave literary records of their interactions. And so when there **is** a historical record of a positive interaction, such as that which took place between St Francis of Assisi and the Mamluk Sultan Malik al-Kamil during the fifth Crusade in 1219, such stories are told repeatedly in a laudable attempt to get a sense of balance in the historical record.[9]

The historian is left to ponder evidence of tragedy and torment. Historians must speak from the evidence before them, not shape the evidence according to today's political whims and desires. There is no doubt that there were centuries of conflict, with Muslim and Christian imperial forces clashing in the process of the inevitable ebb and flow of empires.

### From the centre to the periphery

The patterns of Christian-Muslim interaction were very much set in the Middle East during the first centuries of Islam. As time went on, both faiths expanded to new regions. Let us turn our attention to Southeast Asia, home to around 20% of the world's Muslims.

Although there were travellers who touched on various points of Southeast Asia in the early centuries of Islam for both faiths – often en route for China – the earliest substantial communities of Muslims date from the 13th century. The conversion of rulers to Islam, and thereby their city populations, triggered a process in several phases where Islam gradually expanded through much of the region that we know today as the countries of Malaysia, Indonesia and the Philippines.

Not long after local Southeast Asian communities began to convert en masse to Islam, Christian communities began to spring up in the same region as a result of the arrival of European colonial powers.

---

[9] Cf. Paul Moses, *The Saint and the Sultan: The Crusades, Islam, and Francis of Assisi's Mission of Peace* (Image Press, 2009). Also Philip Kosloski, "St. Francis and the Sultan: An encounter of peace between Christians and Muslims", accessed 16 August 2017,
https://aleteia.org/2017/06/28/st-francis-and-the-sultan-an-encounter-of-peace-between-christians-and-muslims/.

The first to arrive were the Portuguese and Spanish, triggering a process of conversion to Roman Catholicism. They were followed in the early 17th century by the Dutch and the English. Their presence led to much conversion to Protestant Christianity.

It would be wrong to assume that Christians in Southeast Asia grouped together to confront Muslims in Southeast Asia. In fact, often power considerations trumped religious affiliations, with some wars between Muslim states attracting the support of either Catholic or Protestant Christians for one or other of the Muslim sides.

Given that Christians and Muslims in Southeast Asia were establishing relationships hundreds of years after their fellow Christians and Muslims had done the same thing in the Middle East, it is interesting to reflect on how the earlier experience contributed to the shaping of the relationship in Southeast Asia. In fact, it is striking that in many cases Southeast Asian perceptions of the other were strongly influenced by earlier Christian-Muslim interaction.

For example, the Portuguese and Spanish who arrived in Southeast Asia in the 16th century had fresh memories of Christian-Muslim interaction in the Iberian Peninsula from the 8th to the 15th centuries. Much of the interaction in Islamic Spain during the early period had been comfortable, as is emphasised in much modern scholarly writing. But the desire to paint a positive picture among modern historians often overlooks great difficulty during different periods in Spain.

When the Portuguese and Spanish explorers and conquerors in Southeast Asia encountered Muslims, they identified them as hostile "Moors", reflecting their perceptions from earlier centuries. For example, the Portuguese explorer Tome Pires' wrote his 6-volume work *Suma Oriental* after visiting Malacca, Java, Sumatra, and the Moluccas in 1512-15. At the time, Islamic influence was slowly expanding in what had long been a Hindu-Buddhist dominated region. His views of Muslims were essentially negative, writing:

> "The people of Sunda and Java ... keep ... to themselves... The kingdom of Sunda does not allow Moors in it, except for a few, because it is feared that with their cunning they may do there what has been done in Java; because the Moors are

cunning and they make themselves masters of countries by cunning, because apparently they have no power." [10]

Meanwhile, the famous 17th century Muslim scholar from Sumatra, 'Abd al-Ra'uf of Singkel, wrote prolifically on diverse subjects on Islam. One of his works addressed the experience of dying for a Muslim believer. In his account Christians and Jews are presented, along with Satan, as those who tempt the dying person to abandon Islam during the dying process. Demons are portrayed as disguising themselves as relatives of the dying in an attempt to lure the believer away from Islam.

> "Iblis [Satan] orders his soldiers to visit the person at the point of death and to confuse him. So they come to the person at the point of death, and they present themselves to the person in the form of all his loved ones who died before him, of those who guided him during his life, such as his father, mother, brothers, sisters, and friends who cared for him. They say to him: 'O so-and-so. You are dying. We have already undergone the experience of death before you. So please die in the Jewish faith, for it is the faith which is pleasing to Allah.' If the person turns away and does not wish to comply with the urgings of the demons, another group of demons comes to him and says: 'O so-and-so, please die in the Christian faith, for it is the religion of the Messiah, namely Jesus, which through him abrogated the religion of Moses.' These [demons] proceed to list for him all the beliefs of each religion.
>
> Thereupon Allah inclines whoever He wishes towards faiths which have gone astray." [11]

For this work 'Abd al-Ra'uf drew on earlier Muslim writing from the Middle East. This shows the effect of the transmission of negative stereotypes.

Writing a little earlier than the Islamic scholar, the Dutch Governor General in the Netherlands East Indies, Jan Pieterszoon Coen (1587-1629), reinforced negative stereotypes of Muslims, by noting in his memoirs that the Muslims on the island of Ternate and Dutch Christians were "enemies by nature". He observed that these "cruel

---

[10] Tome Pires, *The Suma Oriental of Tome Pires* (London: The Hakluyt Society, 1944), 173.

[11] P. Riddell, "Demonic Temptation in Buddhism and Islam, with particular reference to Southeast Asia", in R. Nicholls & P.G. Riddell (eds), *Faiths in Conversation: Comparative Themes and Perspectives across the Religions*, Occasional Papers in the Study of Islam and Other Faiths No.5 (Melbourne: MST Press, 2015), 103.

and murderous" Muslims were "proud, presumptuous," "deceitful and duplicitous". Islam was "the formidable opponent" of the Dutch, and he strongly opposed Muslims being in "any real alliance with the Dutch."[12]

Sometimes negative perceptions of the other include some curious twists and turns. Consider this portrayal of Christians by Ratu Pakubuwana (d. 1732), the wife of one of the Javanese kings in the early 18th century, who reports God as commenting:

> "O Muhammad ... What distinguishes the Christians is that their arms branch out and they are constantly urinating. ... They use a constant fragrance to conceal their stink. The rotting stink might spread of the bodies of the demons and the Christians (so it is) concealed with fragrance. Enemies of Jesus are these Christians, their forces lions and gibbons and all the demons and demons..."[13]

## Greater Christian awareness

Let us turn our attention back to the present. With such a track record of Christian-Muslim suspicion and negative stereotyping, it is little wonder that Christian-Muslim relations today are complex, to say the least. If Christians and Muslims want to be negative about each other, there is no shortage of material to draw on. But are Christians continuing the negative stereotypes of past centuries under the onslaught of negative media portrayals? Let us now consider the evidence.

In surveying the many questions that have been posed by Christians about Islam in my various public lectures over the years, the first impression is a sense of relief. Unlike the history of Christian views of Islam surveyed earlier which were often based on suspicion, ignorance and misinformation, the questions considered below reflect much more sophisticated and informed approaches by Christian audiences.

In short, the criticism of "the media" supposedly feeding sensationalist viewpoints to the masses about Islam is not borne out

---

[12] Karel Steenbrink, *Dutch Colonialism and Indonesian Islam: Contacts and Conflicts 1596-1950* (Amsterdam: Rodopi, 2006), 60.

[13] Merle Ricklefs, *The Seen and Unseen Worlds in Java, 1726-1749: History, Literature, and Islam in the Court of Pakubuwana II* (St. Leonards, N.S.W.: Asian Studies Association of Australia, 1998), 68.

by my experience of questions from Christian audiences over many years.

The questions can be categorised according to a number of major themes, as follows:

- Muslim plurality
- Christian plurality
- International crises
- Human rights under Islam
- Religion, society and the public discourse
- Spiritual warfare
- Evaluating Islam
- Truth and Christian Muslim relations
- Christian approaches to Islam

## An awareness of diversity

The first discrepancy to note between past Christian views of Islam and present questions by Christians about Islam relates to the issue of an awareness of diversity. The statements cited from past centuries are characterised by a view of Muslims as a monolithic mass. They are described by some of the Christians involved as cunning and deceptive and even as cruel and murderous, without any suggestion in the statements of the diverse nature of Muslim people.

On the other hand, many modern Christians are clearly concerned to understand the diverse nature of Islam. Questions are asked about denominational differences among Muslims. Another favourite question received related to whether radical and more liberal Muslims speak to each other and if so what is the context and what are the outcomes. One question which also crops up on a regular basis is how to decide who are true Muslims, given the vastly different accounts of the Islamic faith given by different Muslim spokespeople. Overall, Christians seem to be aware that all the diverse complexity found within the many expressions of Christianity can also be found among Muslims.

## A search for commonality

Comments by Christian spokespeople in the past have often tended to see Islam and its adherents by default as a rival at best and an enemy at worst. For example, the statement by the Governor General of the Dutch East Indies, Jan Pieterzoon Coen, that Islam was "the formidable opponent" of the Dutch expressed an attitude that was commonplace among Christians in earlier centuries.

By contrast, Christian audiences, while conscious of past conflicts and difficulties in the Christian-Muslim relationship, typically ask questions that are searching for solutions. A common question is "How should Christians respond to the international political crises of the early 21$^{st}$-century?" Also addressed by Christians is whether there is a more helpful mindset to approaching Muslims then just conversion.

### An awareness of sensitivities

Often in the past the language used by Christians to describe Muslims (and indeed the reverse) was crude and bound to offend. In the Song of Roland encountered earlier, the author had no qualms about describing Islam as a pagan idolatry centred upon a demonic Trinity. Indeed, this particular piece of literature was actually incorporated into the French secondary curriculum in the late 19$^{th}$ century.

In the early 21$^{st}$-century, however, Christians are much more inclined to watch their language in engaging with Muslims. A common question received was whether Christians have the right to ask critical questions about core Islamic beliefs. Also of interest to Christian audiences is the question as to how past history and its pattern of conflict should be reported. Another favourite question among Christian audiences is how Christians can interact with Muslim women without causing offence.

### Islam and human rights

A favourite area of Christian questioning in the present day relates to religious minority rights in Muslim-majority locations. While religious liberty advocacy is a feature of the modern era, earlier Christian responses to mistreatment of Christians by Muslims was often characterised by violence, as seen in the Crusades. But in the modern day, Christian audiences like to ask about a Muslim critique of persecution of minorities, showing awareness of diversity among Muslims in seeking a more subtle approach of partnering with friendly Muslims in addressing the problem of persecution of Christians under Islamic rule.

### Religion, society and the public discourse

In certain periods in the past, Christians have been reluctant to make space for Muslim minorities. Indeed, both Muslims and Jews were expelled from different parts of Europe in some of the darker phases of the history of Christendom.

However today Christians, through their questioning, are seeking ways to respond to requests for mosques to be built in neighbourhoods. Christians also ask questions about whether Islamic political advocacy has opened the door for greater Christian involvement in the public square. Also striking is the preparedness of Christians to work with people of other faiths in facing the common challenge of secularism, as indicated by a range of related questions.

### Evaluating Islam

In the past, Christian spokespeople who commented on Islam tended to speak in black-and-white terms as seen in the statements presented earlier. Today's Christian audiences seek to resolve inconsistent messages about the nature of Islam. A favourite question is "Is Islam a religion of peace?" Another is "Is terrorism more likely to flow out of Islam than Christianity?"

Another stark distinction between past and present in Christian attitudes relates to openness to reading the Islamic primary texts. Translations of the Qur'an into vernacular languages in the West is a relatively recent phenomenon and few Westerners studied Islam or read its sacred texts in earlier periods. A common question from Christian audiences today is whether and how Christians should read the Qur'an. This willingness among the masses to engage sacred literature of another faith is a feature of the late 20$^{th}$/early 21$^{st}$ century that has few parallels in earlier history.

### Christian approaches to Islam

Perhaps the starkest distinction between attitudes from the past and the present among Christians relates to a willingness to approach Islam and Muslims with a mindset of openness and friendship. While it is difficult to gather evidence of individual friendships from earlier centuries, making a direct comparison impossible, it is highly likely that today's more open societies and greater communications offer opportunities for Christian-Muslim friendship that did not exist before. This is reflected in the kinds of questions Christian audiences are asking. "What are the best ways to do Interfaith dialogue?" is a common question. Also of interest are questions asking how Christians can pray for and with Muslims.

## Conclusion

We therefore return to the original statement made at the outset of this paper. Is it true that mass media portrayals are causing widespread ignorance, misunderstanding and misrepresentation about the faith of Islam among Western audiences. On the evidence available in public lectures which I have given and the questions received in those lectures, my conclusion is that such an assertion is not correct in terms of Christian audiences. What comes through very clearly in reviewing and assessing questions from Christian audiences is the degree to which their questions are nuanced, revealing a level of understanding that is encouraging. Furthermore, such well-informed Christian audiences usually bring a spirit of openness to the differences that Islam represents, as well as a willingness to seek positive ways of engaging with Muslims.

Christians may have fought wars with Muslims century after century in earlier times. Those wars shaped attitudes that were based on suspicion and misapprehension. But Christians have come a long way on the evidence before me in my interactions with public audiences. While there is more work to be done, we can celebrate the fine balance that has been achieved among Christians between openness and respect towards Muslims while still maintaining a sense of purpose in reaching out to them with the message of the Gospel.

# Muslim Plurality

### Does Islam have denominations like Christianity?

With this question, it is helpful to begin by drawing a distinction between Islam as a religious system and Muslims as people: the people who follow the faith of Islam. The religious system of Islam serves as a kind of glue that binds diverse Muslim people together.

Muslims are certainly as divided as are Christians. Usually we don't talk about denominations within Islam but we often talk about sectarian differences. There is a fundamental division between two main groups: Sunnis and Shi'a. They represent about 85% and 15% respectively of Muslims worldwide.

Then within each of those two Muslim groups there are huge differences according to doctrinal interpretation, approaches to law, fundamentalist and more modernist kinds of thinking, literalist compared with highly mystical groups, and so forth. Various labels are used by people who study Islam to describe different kinds of Muslims: modernist, liberal, moderate, traditionalist, radical, Salafi, Wahhabi, Isma'ili, and lots of other categories. Many Muslims among both Sunni and Shi'i groups are inclined towards Sufi mysticism, belonging to one or more of a number of Sufi orders. Formal group categories are summarised in the following table.

| Ahmadiyya | Sunni | | Shi'a | | Khawarij |
|---|---|---|---|---|---|
| Shafi'i | Hanbali | Twelver | Jafari | | Ibadi |
| Hanafi | Maliki | Isma'ili | Sevener | | Alevi |
| Barelvi | Deobandi | Druze | Alawi | | Zaydi |
| Wahhabi | Salafi | Bohra | Nizari | | Akbari |
| Sufi | Qadiri | Naqshbandi | Chishti | | Shadhili |

So Muslim people are incredibly divided. But they all share the same Qur'an and they also look to Muhammad as the prophetic model of their faith, drawing on collections of traditions about his statements and deeds, known as the Hadith.

## Are there serious dialogues between radical Muslims and other Muslims?

This question can be related to two of the most prominent manifestations of radical Islamic activity in the 21st century: the 9/11 attacks and the rapid expansion of the Islamic State in Iraq and Syria from 2014.

Barely one month after the 9/11 terrorist attacks in New York and Washington DC, a gathering of Muslim scholars in Europe meeting on 16 October 2001 denounced the al-Qaeda network that had carried out the attacks:

> "The so-called Qaeda Organization… is not in any way an Islamic organization and its activities should not be linked to Muslims. The statements of the spokesmen of this organization are not in keeping with the teachings of Islam and have nothing to do with the Sunna. Not one of the leaders of this group enjoy the attributes that give him the right to issue fatwas…"[14]

In response, al-Qaeda leader Osama Bin Laden responded to such statements rejecting his Islamic credentials by doing some rejections of his own:

> "The fatwa of any official aalim (religious figure) has no value for me. History is full of such ulema (clerics) who justify Riba (interest), who justify the occupation of Palestine by the Jews, who justify the presence of American troops around Harmain Sharifain (holy places in Saudi Arabia). These people support the infidels for their personal gain. The true ulema support the jihad against America."[15]

Over a decade later, the forces of Islamic State conquered swathes of territory in Syria and Iraq, slaughtering and enslaving Shi'a Muslims, Yazidis and Christians wherever they went and justifying their methods as *jihad* in the cause of Allah. In response, an open letter endorsed by hundreds of prominent Islamic leaders and scholars around the world was addressed to Islamic State leaders, bitterly condemning their actions. The lengthy document included the

---

[14] *Al-Hayāh*, October 23, 2001, cited in Arab West Report, "A Statement by the Muslim Scholars in Europe", 23 October, 2001, accessed 10 July, 2017, http://www.arabwestreport.info/en/year-2001/week-43/18-statement-muslim-scholars-europe.

[15] "Muslims have the right to attack America," 11 November, 2001, accessed 15 May, 2017, https://www.theguardian.com/world/2001/nov/11/terrorism.afghanistan1.

following injunctions referring specifically to the religious minorities that suffered heavily under Islamic State:

> 10. It is forbidden in Islam to harm or mistreat—in any way—Christians or any 'People of the Scripture'.
>
> 11. It is obligatory to consider Yazidis as People of the Scripture.[16]

These exchanges provide good examples of the typical relationship between radical and more mainstream voices within the worldwide Islamic community. They usually talk past each other, with the result that meaningful dialogue between radicals and the more moderate mainstream is rare.

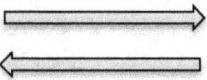

In such cases, when Muslim radicals and moderates dismiss each other's credentials as Muslims, a related question arises.

### Should Christians make a decision as to who are real Muslims?

When witnessing such intra-Muslim debates, it is tempting for outsiders to adjudicate by identifying which of the Muslim parties in dispute represent "real Islam".

Christian Evangelicals, with their firm commitment to scripture as the ultimate yardstick of theological orthodoxy, tend to apply the same criteria in evaluating Muslims. Thus Muslim radicals are often seen by Christian evangelicals (especially those at the more fundamentalist end of the evangelical spectrum) as "real Muslims" because of their scriptural-literalist approach. However, this response really represents more of a window into the mind of the Christians concerned than of the Muslims they claim to comment on.

Christians should avoid passing judgement in such intra-Muslim debates. It is up to Muslims to define their community membership and resolve their differences. While Christians may hope that certain views will prevail in intra-Muslim arguments, it is not up to

---

[16] "Open letter to Dr. Ibrahm Awwad Al-Badri, alias 'Abu Bakr Al-Baghdadi' and to the fighters and followers of the self-declared 'Islamic state'," 24th Dhul-Qi'da 1435 AH/19th September 2014 CE, accessed 13 May, 2017, http://www.lettertobaghdadi.com.

Christians to adjudicate, declaring group X or group Y as the "real Muslims".

## So what is Islam?[17]

There are many faces to Islam and the people who embrace it. The diversity of Islam is reflected in a Hui Chinese peasant popping occasionally into his mosque, which resembles a pagoda and has the Islamic Creed (*shahada*) on the wall in Chinese, not Arabic. Islam is equally a Javanese villager going straight from Friday prayers to the rice fields where he will leave an offering to the Goddess of the rice, Dewi Sri.

Islam is also a Lombok folk Muslim who once told me in conversation that Islam only has three pillars, not five. Islam is equally the Iranian gentleman I met one evening in a street café by the Caspian Sea who wasn't the least bit interested in answering my questions about his faith but preferred to talk about the last time Iran played Australia in soccer.

> *Islamist radicals only represent one face of the mosaic that is Islam.*

Islam is the faith of prominent modernisers such as Anwar Ibrahim, Mohammad Arkoun, Mohammad Talbi, Nurcholish Madjid, Benazir Bhutto and others who are outspokenly critical of Islamist radicals, who argue for a separation between mosque and state, and who want to develop an updated Islamic hermeneutic.

And Islam is also represented by Islamist radicals, who will point to the Islamic primary texts ... indeed will dwell on those texts ... and say that other Muslims such as those above are not true Muslims. But such a response itself only represents one face of the mosaic that is Islam.

Yet a mosaic represents both diversity and unity, with varied expressions that are held together by an underlying framework. In the case of Islam, this framework is provided by Muhammad as model, and the texts (Qur'an and Hadith) that emerged from his life,

---

[17] The views expressed in this paragraph reflect my engagement with Muslims in vastly different contexts around the world over several decades.

and the Shariah legal system that systematises and regularises Muslim life.

# Christian Plurality

**Do Christian denominational divisions provide fuel for some Muslims who seek to discredit Christians and their faith?**

There is a widespread perception among Muslims that Christians are hopelessly divided. This is reinforced by specific references within the Qur'an, such as the following:

> *Q98:4 Nor did the People of the Book become divided until after there came to them clear evidence.*
>
> *Q5:14 And from those who say, "We are Christians" We[1] took their covenant; but they forgot a portion of that of which they were reminded. So We caused among them animosity and hatred until the Day of Resurrection. And Allah is going to inform them about what they used to do.*

In explaining Q98:4, the famous commentator Yusuf Ali suggests that the fragmentation among the People of the Book[2] is a direct result of having rejected the message of Islam.[3] Thus the great schism between Orthodoxy and Catholicism in the 11th century, and the later Catholic-Protestant divisions, are considered to represent the fruit of having rejected Islam centuries before.

In this context, continuing public bickering along Christian denominational lines is seen by many Muslims as further evidence of modern Christianity's lack of validity as a revealed faith. Thus Christians who cannot build bridges among themselves cannot hope to successfully reach out to Muslims en masse.

**What is the general Muslim perception of Christianity and vice-versa?**

There is no such thing as a "general perception". Some Muslims view Christianity positively, admiring its piety, while others view it as

---

[1] Allah is speaking as "We".

[2] Primarily Christians and Jews.

[3] Abdullah Yusuf Ali, *The Meaning of the Holy Qur'an*, New ed. (Beltsville, Maryland: Amana Publications, 1989), 1768, n. 6227.

debased and corrupt, often equating Christianity with the decadence of the modern secular West.

A view commonly held by Muslims is that expressed by Shagufta Yaqub, British journalist and commentator and former editor of the prominent Muslim monthly *Q-News*, who made the following comment in interview:

> "I see most Christians – or, at least, people who were born into a Christian family – as having come very far from their religious beliefs. When I think of the church, I think of it as such a loose thing now... Christianity has tried so hard to stay alive by changing with the times, it's lost a lot of its original message."[4]

Ms Yaqub has clearly picked up on the widely varying messages coming from different Christian groups, ranging from all-embracing pluralists at one end of a long spectrum who see diverse paths leading to the one heavenly goal, to narrow fundamentalists at the other who preach a highly restricted access to salvation.

For example, some Christian pluralists are willing to argue for a measure of divine involvement in the life and ministry of Muhammad, Messenger of Islam, and the texts which are associated with him. Dr Clinton Bennett, Anglican priest and scholar, writes that:

> "I do not know *how* the Qur'an was communicated by God through Muhammad, but I can accept that it was; as I view the incarnation as a mystery, so I view the *bookification* of the Qur'an."[5]

In similar vein, Fr. Ovey N. Mohammed, a Jesuit priest, declares:

> "... Muhammad had a prophetic charism that enabled him to communicate some fundamental and biblical truths about God and human beings... if Muhammad was a prophet in some sense, then the Qur'an is certainly *a* word of God."[6]

---

[4] "Two Sides of a Different Coin? Anthony McRoy talks to Sheikh Omar Bakri Muhammad and Shagufta Yaqub," *Third Way*, March 2003, 21.

[5] Clinton Bennett, *In Search of Muhammad* (London & New York: Cassell, 1998), 236.

[6] Ovey N. Mohammed, *Muslim-Christian Relations: Past, Present, Future* (Maryknoll: Orbis Books, 1999), 64-65.

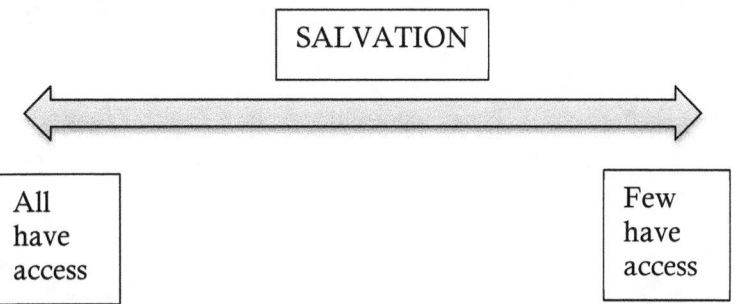

However, such pluralist views are to be found on the margins of Christianity. Most Christians would not support such pluralist statements, and would consider that any recognition of the Qur'an as divinely-sourced and of Muhammad as a genuine prophet would be tantamount to accepting Islam's claims as the final revelation, thereby superseding Christianity and its unique message.

# International Crises

## How central is the Israel Issue to Christian-Muslim relations around the world?

Analysis of this much-discussed issue is driven in large part by different perspectives and angles on the Israeli-Palestinian conflict.

Many Muslims incorrectly assume the establishment of the State of Israel in 1948 was an attempt to reassert European colonial control via a latter-day Crusader state. M. Shahid Alam expresses this in condemning suggestions that Pakistan might recognise Israel:

> "...if Zengi,[1] Nur al-Din, Salahuddin and the Egyptian Mamluks refused to recognize the Crusader states, can Muslims today be expected to choose differently?"[2]

Furthermore, many Muslims see European and American economic and military links with Israel since its creation as evidence of the West's expansionist goals. The humiliating defeat of Arab armies by Israel in several wars since 1948 is thus considered to have been facilitated by the West.

Many non-Muslims challenge such views as over-simplifications of a very complex conflict. Many argue that the historical presence of a Jewish community in the Holy Land for thousands of years entitles the Jews to a state, on part of the land at least. It is further pointed out that Western, and indeed, American support for Israel is not monolithic. Furthermore, Muslim perspectives tend to ignore how Palestinian and other Arab actions and policies have contributed to the intractable nature of the conflict over the years. Moreover, they also ignore the very vigorous debate within Israeli society concerning policies vis-à-vis its Arab neighbours.

Nevertheless, from a Muslim perspective, support for the Israeli-Palestinian peace process among Palestinians in the West Bank and Gaza based on a two-state solution is in decline, down from 52% in

---

[1] Imad ad-Din Zengi (1087-1146). Cf. Carole Hillenbrand, *The Crusades: Islamic Perspectives* (New York: Routledge, 2000), 112-16.

[2] M. Shahid Alam, "Pakistan 'Recognizes' Israel," accessed 7 September, 2003, http://www.khilafah.com/home/category.php?DocumentID=8225&TagID=2. See also David Ohana, "Are Israelis the New Crusaders?," *The Palestine-Israel Journal,* 13, no. 3, 2006, http://www.pij.org/details.php?id=865.

June 2014 to 44% three years later. At the same time support for rejectionist radical Islamist solutions to the conflict has also declined but remains worryingly strong, with 41% of Palestinian respondents choosing the liberation of all of Palestine in June 2001 and 18% choosing this option in 2017.[3] Clearly for many Palestinians, and this is echoed by Muslim masses in other countries, a two-state solution would be a sell-out of Palestinian rights. Many prefer for Israel to disappear as a state, as they consider it to be an alien Western implant in the Muslim heartlands.

## So is the conflict surrounding the state of Israel a root cause of Islamic radicalism?

The response must be a clear NO. While the conflict fuels the radical Islamist movement, it is not a root cause. Islamic radical ideologies have existed since the 7th century, long before the establishment of the state of Israel in 1948. Moreover, if Israel ceased to exist tomorrow, Muslim radicals would find other arenas of conflict where military engagement was seen as appropriate: Chechnya, the Sudan, Kashmir, the Southern Philippines, Indonesia, to name a few.

> *If Israel ceased to exist tomorrow, Muslim radicals would find other arenas of conflict where military engagement was seen as appropriate.*

In the words of the radical British Muslim group Al-Muhajiroun:

> "Muslims will proclaim that the only solution to the atrocities being committed against them in Palestine, Kashmir, Chechnya or Afghanistan is Jihad; an obligation to engage in physically upon those nearest and an obligation upon the Muslims around the world to support verbally, financially and physically!"[4]

In essence (and this is key), the radicals' literalist reading of Islamic scripture leads them to conclude that non-believers (that is, non-Muslims) are "infidels" and should be fought. They draw their inspiration from Qur'anic verses such as the following: "Fight and slay the Pagans wherever ye find them, and seize them, beleaguer

---

[3] D. Polisar, "Do Palestinians Want a Two-State Solution?," *Mosaic*, April 3, 2017, https://mosaicmagazine.com/essay/2017/04/do-palestinians-want-a-two-state-solution/.

[4] "Press Release," 7 November, 2001, accessed 7 September, 2003, http://www.almuhajiroun.com.

them, and lie in wait for them in every stratagem," (Surah 9, verse 5). The issue of Israel is more a manifestation of the radicals' conflict with the West, rather than a root cause.[5]

However, it should be noted that many, perhaps most, Muslims would disagree with this assessment, opting to identify Israel as the root cause of diverse conflicts in the Middle East. Such a view of Israel is also shared by many Europeans. An October 2003 opinion poll conducted by the Eurobarometer organisation and based on interviews with 500 people in each of the 15 states of the European Union found that 59% of those surveyed considered Israel to be the greatest threat to world peace, followed closely by the United States and North Korea in joint second place.[6] A late 2013 poll of 66,000 people in 65 countries found the USA to be the greatest threat to world peace, with Israel coming in 4$^{th}$ place.[7]

It seems that Muslim views on this particular issue find considerable support among the masses of the European Union and beyond, where the centuries-long history of popular anti-Semitism morphs on occasions into popular attitudes to the State of Israel.

## How should Christians respond to the international political crises of the early 21$^{st}$ century?

There are various elements to a right response which Christians should consider. At the outset it is important to sift critically through a mass of issues, distinguishing the primary from the secondary.

Issues such as the diversity of Muslim opinion and the need to condemn anti-Muslim public reaction are important and require a response. However they are, in a key sense, secondary to the central issue, from which our attention must not be deflected.

The fact is that there are international networks of radical Muslims committed to terrorism and to disrupting the international order that must be stopped. These networks, including groups such as Al-

---

[5] For a detailed discussion of the origins of anti-Western feeling in the Muslim world, c.f. Peter G. Riddell and Peter Cotterell, *Islam in Context: Past, Present and Future* (Grand Rapids, 2003), chapter 10.

[6] "EU embarrassed as poll labels Israel world's biggest threat," 3 November, 2003, accessed 20 December, 2003,
http://story.news.yahoo.com/news?tmpl=story&u=/afp/20031103/wl_mideast_afp/eu_pol1_israel_031103172948.

[7] "US is the greatest threat to world peace: poll," *New York Post,* January 5, 2014,
http://nypost.com/2014/01/05/us-is-the-greatest-threat-to-world-peace-poll/.

Qaeda, the Islamic State of Iraq and Syria, Boko Haram in Africa, Jemaah Islamiyah in the countries of Southeast Asia, and a plethora of other groups, have come into public view since September 11th, 2001, but they were far from dormant prior to that date.

Christians need to acknowledge from the outset that Islamic radicalism must be confronted through swift and effective action of various kinds.

First, then, churches should be encouraged to increase their contacts with modernising Muslims at times of crisis. This can be done through engaging in dialogue at the community level, forming individual friendships, partnering in social issues, as well as offering hospitality to Muslim neighbours or colleagues.

Second, Christian leaders should support government efforts to distinguish publicly between different kinds of Muslims. Clearly many Muslims do not support and therefore do not bear responsibility for terrorist attacks such as the wave of strikes on European civilian targets in recent years. Also important to acknowledge, however, is a third group of Muslims who may not personally take part in terror strikes but nevertheless sympathise with such action and do not report to authorities on planned attacks.[8]

Third, and in recognition of the fact that Western governments and allied states need to take appropriate action against the radical Islamic groups, Christian leaders should give support to government moves to strengthen anti-terrorist legislation, arrest and detention, and appropriate military action.[9] Such measures received the sanction of the United Nations Security Council on 28 September 2001 when it adopted a wide-ranging, comprehensive resolution with steps and strategies to combat international terrorism.[10]

---

[8] The existence of such a phenomenon is borne out by surveys of Muslim communities. Cf. Peter G. Riddell, "Britain Pays the Price for Complacency," *American Spectator,* June 6, 2017, https://spectator.org/britain-pays-the-price-for-complacency/.

[9] I agree with Garlow, who writes: "On occasion, war is the correct course of action. Failure to act leads to increasingly more acts of random, massive terrorism worldwide. And yes, Christians can support their nation in war. While I respect those who are pacifists, I believe their position is naïve regarding the profound depths of original sin and its containment and naïve regarding the authority that God grants to the civil authority to deal with those who disrupt and harm society." James L. Garlow, *A Christian's response to Islam* (Eastbourne, UK: Kingsway, 2005), 120.

[10] "UN Security Council Resolution 1373," 2001, accessed 30 April, 2003, http://www.un.org/News/Press/docs/2001/sc7158.doc.htm.

Fourth, Christian leaders should encourage their governments to seek partnerships with moderate Muslim governments in the ongoing response to the radicals. Furthermore, efforts to draw together and maintain broad coalitions, including Muslim nations, such as the coalition against Islamic State in Iraq and Syria, provide hope in a time of international crisis. The present troubles should not be allowed to morph into a general conflict between the West and Islam.

Fifth, Christian leaders should advise caution about calls to negotiate with radical jihadi Islamists. Such a well-intentioned but naive call was made in April 2004 by former Northern Ireland Secretary Mo Mowlam, who urged the British and American governments to open talks with Osama bin Laden and al-Qaeda around a negotiating table.[11] The fact is that Muslim radicals are driven by a literalist reading of Islamic scripture which leads them to conclude that non-Muslims are "infidels" and should be fought; such groups would see negotiations merely as a stratagem towards their ultimate goals.

A sixth and essential step in identifying right responses to the current world crisis involves turning to the pages of the Bible for wisdom and guidance. The responses outlined above are eclectic, combining irenic approaches with measured support for the use of force. This conforms to Biblical standards. In Matthew's Gospel, Jesus told his disciples to turn the other cheek when struck,[12] but later in the same book he also overturned forcefully the tables of the moneychangers in the Temple.[13] In other words, we need to select our response wisely, according to circumstance: sometimes dialogue and humility will be the best course, but on other occasions a more forceful response (when the former does not bring about a Godly environment) will be required.

---

[11] "'Negotiate with Bin Laden': Mowlam," *Guardian* April 8, 2004.

[12] Matthew 5:39. See also Luke 6:29.

[13] Matthew 21:12. See also Mark 11:15 and John 2:15. Admittedly these passages record the use of force against objects and animals, not against people. But it could be argued that the biblical sanctioning of force, even under restricted conditions, opens up the possibility of its use under broader circumstances, on condition that the pursuit of justice be the over-riding motivation.

## Is Christianity more supportive of globalisation, industrialisation, and capitalism than Islam?

Christianity is not inherently more supportive of globalisation than Islam. Many Muslim writers condemn globalisation, but a close reading of their writings shows that they are not opposed to globalisation per se, arguing rather for localism or regionalism. On the contrary, these writers are typically driven by a desire for Islamic globalisation, promoting Islamic banks around the world, seeking to empower the Organisation of Islamic Conference which includes over fifty Muslim nations in a kind of mini-UN, and urging Islamic women around the world to stop wearing jeans and to don the head-cover. That is globalisation under a different guise.

> Many Muslim writers condemn globalisation, but they are not opposed to globalisation per se, but are typically driven by a desire for Islamic globalisation.

Likewise for industrialisation. Muslims of most varieties are in favour of economic progress, for which a prerequisite is industrialisation. The concern of many is not with industrialisation per se, but rather that it should seek to advance the Islamisation of society. Malaysia is a classic case in point. It made massive strides in industrialisation during the second half of the 20th century with the development of its oil and gas, palm oil, rubber and ore mining industries. This period also witnessed the promotion of Islamisation both from above (by the governments) and at the grassroots level.

As for capitalism, there certainly are aspects of capitalism which go against the grain of Islamic economic theory. The obvious one is the use of interest on loans for financing further economic activity. But such details aside, there are many Muslim-majority countries around the world which seek Islamisation within a largely capitalist framework. Such Islamic capitalism is packaged under a range of different brands: halal certification, Shariah banking, Islamic economics, and so forth. Malaysia is again a good example.

## Is a clash between the West and Islam inevitable?

There is certainly a great potential for ongoing rivalry between the Western and Islamic worlds. Islam is a total package for life. It is far more than simply a faith for Friday worship; in addition to covering theology and doctrine, Islam offers a powerful set of Shariah legal codes, guidelines for economic organisation, principles of political involvement, strict social and moral guidelines, and precepts in wide-ranging domains. In contrast, the West vigorously enforces a separation between sacred and secular. It is difficult to reconcile these fundamentally different Islamic and Western approaches.

Moreover, Islamic doctrine is most comfortable when its adherents constitute the majority in society, and Islamic law assumes that situation. Muslim minorities in Western countries have proven to be some of the most awkward minorities, with some members reluctant to cohere with majority non-Muslim society. Muslim minority spokespeople often argue that relational difficulties with the non-Muslim majority is due largely to exclusion and alienation.[14] However, there are far deeper issues in play, in terms of inbuilt rivalry and competition between Western and Islamic ideologies.

Nevertheless, rivalry need not turn to conflict if carefully handled, with goodwill on both sides. Rivalry can be good; conflict is rarely good.

## Do Muslims welcome non-Muslim campaigns against terrorism?[15]

The world's focus on the Middle East since 2011 has fallen on the tragic results of the Syrian Civil War. Much of that attention has been preoccupied by the jihad campaigns of the Islamic State in Iraq and Syria since 2014, and their tactics of mass killings, beheadings and enslavement of their opponents.

The world has forgotten that this reign of terror by Islamic State was foreshadowed over a decade earlier in the same region. In 2002 Dr Hedieh Mirahmadi, a prominent representative of the Sufi-inclined Islamic Supreme Council of America (ISCA), wrote an article in the *National Review Online* (NRO),[16] in which she expressed deep concerns about the activities of radical Muslims, whom she termed

---

[14] Cf. Aminul Hoque, "Young British Muslims alienated by 'us versus them' rhetoric of counter-terrorism," *The Conversation,* September 29, 2017,
http://theconversation.com/young-british-muslims-alienated-by-us-versus-them-rhetoric-of-counter-terrorism-46117.

[15] An earlier version of the discussion in this section appeared as "Why Not All Muslims Support the Radicals," *Church Times* 3 January, 2003, 11.

[16] Hedieh Mirahmadi, "Jihadi Tomb Raiders," *National Review,* December 13, 2002, http://old.nationalreview.com/comment/comment-mirahmadi121302.asp.

"jihadis", who had set up a mini Islamic state in the mountains on the Iraq-Iran border around a dozen Kurdish villages. They had received funding and weaponry from Osama Bin Laden's al-Qaeda, as well as increased fighting strength from jihadi warriors who had fled Afghanistan with the fall of the Taliban in 2001.

These jihadis desecrated ancient Sufi tombs that had served as sites of local pilgrimage for inhabitants of the region for centuries. In a particularly gruesome development, the radicals stole corpses of revered saints from these tombs, beheading them in the streets as a mark of defiance of local custom. Furthermore, a blanket ban was placed on any public or private display of photos of deceased relatives and living friends and families. Restrictions on the public movement of women were applied through a set of edicts.

Such radical activity adheres to a well-established pattern. In her article Mirahmadi points to the depths of its roots in saying that "these extremists follow a 200-year-old radical doctrine that has brought only injustice, oppression, and violence to those brought under its sway." The most recent manifestation is, of course, the murderous Islamic State group who swept through eastern Syria and western Iraq in 2014.

The ISCA represents one prominent Muslim group with a considerable international Muslim support base which debunks the myth of Muslim solidarity in opposition to America and the West. This particular Muslim group consistently calls on the West to act in confronting the Muslim radical networks. Mirahmadi warned in her article that "if the West remains silent while these militants conquer centuries-old communities of devout yet moderate Muslims, then they will continue to spread."

Mirahmadi was clearly at odds with both Muslim and Western commentators who, in the wake of the 9/11 attacks, insisted that American foreign policy was the ultimate source of international tensions.[17] She insisted that "the greatest danger to the freedoms of Muslims everywhere in the world, including the U.S., is not the war on terror, but the oppression and intolerance of radicals who continue to commit atrocities in the name of religion."

---

[17] For an analysis of such comments, c.f. Riddell and Cotterell, *Islam in Context: Past, Present and Future*, chapter 10.

Over 15 years later, fierce debates continue to rage among Western commentators over the best method to respond to the challenge of radical Islam. We should be reminded of similar debates taking place among Muslims themselves.[18] In this context, bridge-building with such moderate Muslim groups is a necessity.

## Is there a link between terrorism and refugees?

This is an especially sensitive question given the vast flows of refugees entering Europe from diverse sources from 2014 onwards. The answer to this question is both no and yes.

> *Fierce debates continue to rage among Western commentators over the best method to respond to the challenge of radical Islam. Bridge-building with moderate Muslim groups is a necessity.*

It should be noted that although the majority of refugees reaching European shores from 2014 were Muslim, there were nevertheless many non-Muslim refugees, especially Christians and Yazidis, none of whom were associated with terrorist strikes on European targets. So associating terrorism with refugees as a blanket statement is false, as non-Muslim refugees should be exonerated of such an association.

Equally the vast majority of Muslim refugees were not associated with any of the terrorist strikes against European targets such as occurred in Manchester, Paris, Nice, Berlin, Brussels and so forth. So the first answer to the question must be that there is no automatic link between terrorism and refugees.

At the same time, the answer to the question also needs to be partly in the affirmative. Firstly, all of the above-mentioned terror strikes were carried out by Muslims, some of whom had entered Europe as refugees according to available evidence.[19]

---

[18] Cf. "Muslims debate 'radical Islam' at Senate hearing", *Washington Examiner,* June 28, 2016, http://www.washingtonexaminer.com/muslims-debate-radical-islam-at-senate-hearing/article/2595166.

[19] "Two of the Stade de France attackers [November 2015] were carrying Syrian passports… the fingerprints and photos of the attackers do clearly match those taken at a refugee registration centre in Greece…" Marco Funk and Roderick Parkes, "Refugees versus terrorists," Issue Alert no. 6, (European Union Institute for Security Studies, January 2016), 1, http://www.iss.europa.eu/uploads/media/Alert_6_Refugees_versus_terrorists.pdf.

What is more difficult to quantify but nevertheless needs to be stated is that where Muslim refugee communities cluster together in camps or ghettos, they become targets for radical Islamist recruitment by groups such as Al-Qaeda and ISIS.[20] In such circumstances, growing support for and involvement in terrorist activity is a risk among expanding Muslim refugee communities in European locations.

---

[20] Scott Gerwehr and Sara Daly, "Al-Qaida: Terrorist Selection and Recruitment," in *The McGraw-Hill Homeland Security Handbook: The Definitive Guide for Law Enforcement, EMT, and all other Security Professionals* (New York: McGraw-Hill, 2005), 81.

# Human Rights under Islam[1]

Much attention within Christian circles is devoted to the treatment of Christian minority communities in Muslim-majority locations. This receives regular attention from Christian churches and other bodies engaged in religious liberty advocacy,[2] leading to frequent questioning by Christians such as the following question posed at the 2003 London Lectures:

> "One is free to become a Muslim, but not free to leave Islam. How is it possible to have a two-way dialogue with a partner that is not willing to reconsider his own point of view; i.e. when freedom is only available to one of the dialogue partners?"

There are significant differences between Islam and Christianity regarding conversion away from one's original faith. If a Christian renounces Christianity and becomes a Muslim, his/her family and community would probably be disappointed. There may be some negative comments made, or in the most extreme cases the convert may be disowned by his/her family. However, there is no severe religious prohibition as such on conversion away from Christianity.

In contrast, Islamic law does not allow for Muslims to renounce their faith. The punishment for apostasy according to Islamic Law is severe. While "some modernists have argued against the traditional death penalty for apostasy on the grounds that the Qur'an only specifies other-worldly punishment",[3] in more conservative or remote Islamic locations capital punishment is still sometimes implemented, both by officialdom and by radical Islamists.[4]

The Universal Declaration of Human Rights specifies at Article 18 that:

> "Everyone has the right to freedom of thought, conscience and religion; this right includes freedom to change his religion or

---

[1] Cf. also Vinoth Ramachandra, *Faiths in Conflict?: Christian Integrity in a Multicultural World* (USA: IVP Academic, 2000), 30-34.

[2] Cf. the work of the Barnabas Fund http://www.barnabasfund.org, Christian Solidarity Worldwide http://www.csw.org.uk, and Middle East Concern http://www.meconcern.org/.

[3] Kate Zebiri, *Muslims and Christians Face to Face* (Oxford: Oneworld Publications, 1997), 29. Cf. Abdullah Saeed, *Freedom of Religion, Apostasy and Islam* (London: Routledge, 2004).

[4] Consider the case of Mahmoud Mohammed Taha, tried and executed for apostasy from Islam in 1985 in Sudan.

belief, and freedom, either alone or in community with others and in public or private, to manifest his religion or belief in teaching, practice, worship and observance."[5]

Human rights agencies and certain national governments have lobbied hard for widespread implementation of this provision in recent decades. These efforts have led to an increasing openness in traditionally Christian countries in the West to expanded worship and missionary activities by non-Christian faiths.

However, Muslim majority countries have resisted full implementation of this provision, even those which are signatories to the Universal Declaration of Human Rights. Their opposition is due to a range of factors: guidelines laid down relating to apostasy in Islamic scripture and legal texts, recent legislation drawn up by governments in some Muslim countries, and unwillingness by Muslim populations to countenance the spread of non-Muslim faiths in Muslim lands.

> Olayemi, Alabi and Buang (2015): "Muslims recognize no authority or power but that of Almighty God and that there is not any legal tradition apart from Islamic law."

Indeed, alternative declarations on Human Rights have been issued by various Islamic authorities: the Universal Islamic Declaration of Human Rights (UIDHR), 1981, and the Cairo Declaration of Human Rights in Islam (CDHRI), 1990. The spirit of these documents is encapsulated well in a 2015 study in the *Journal of Islam, Law and Judiciary*, where the authors state "Muslims recognize no authority or power but that of Almighty God and that there is not any legal tradition apart from Islamic law."[6]

---

[5] "Universal Declaration of Human Rights," accessed 16 May, 2017, http://www.un.org/en/universal-declaration-human-rights/.

[6] Abdul Azeez Maruf Olayemi, Abdul Majeed Hamzah Alabi and Ahmad Hidayah Buang, "Islamic Human Rights Law: A Critical Evaluation of UIDHR & CDHRI in Context of UDHR", *Journal of Islam, Law and Judiciary*, no. 1 (2015): 31.

## Teachings in Islamic Scripture

The Qur'an, the ultimate scriptural authority of Islam and believed by Muslims to be the Word of God, has the following to say about those who abandon Islam for another faith:

> *Those who turn back as apostates after Guidance was clearly shown to them - the Evil One has instigated them and buoyed them up with false hopes. (Q47:25)*

The second most authoritative scriptural source within Islam, the prophetic Traditions or Hadith, has the following to say about apostasy:

> *Narrated `Abdullah: Allah's Apostle said, 'The blood of a Muslim who confesses that none has the right to be worshipped but Allah and that I am His Apostle, cannot be shed except in three cases: In Qisas for murder, a married person who commits illegal sexual intercourse and the one who reverts from Islam (apostate) and leaves the Muslims.'*[7]

Islamic law schools, both Sunni (Hanafi, Shafi'i, Hanbali and Maliki) and Shi'i, drew on such statements in the Qur'an and Hadith to formulate precise guidelines for punishing those guilty of apostasy. Thus the above Hadith reference is incorporated in the legal text *al-Risala* of the Maliki Law School as follows:

> "... An apostate is ... killed unless he repents. He is allowed three days grace; if he fails to utilise the chance to repent, the execution takes place. This same also applies to women apostates."[8]

The legal texts prescribed that apostates were to undergo other punishments prior to the application of the death sentence. This is again specified in *al-Risala*:

---

[7] Bukhari vol. 9, book 83, no 17, accessed 29 July, 2017, https://sunnah.com/bukhari/87. Cf. Muhammed ibn Ismaiel Al-Bukhari, *Sahih al-Bukhari: the translation of the meanings of Sahih al-Bukhari: Arabic-English* trans. Muhammad Muhsin Khan, 9 vols., vol. 9 (Riyadh: Darussalam, 1997), 20.

[8] 'Abdullah Ibn Abi Zayd Al-Qayrawani, "The Risala: A Treatise on Maliki Fiqh," accessed 16 May, 2017, http://www.iiu.edu.my/deed/lawbase/risalah_maliki/. Section 37.19 Crimes Against Islam. Cf. 'Abd Allah ibn 'Abd al-Rahman Ibn Abi Zayd al-Qayrawani, *Al-Risala* (London: Ta-Ha, 1999).

"If either of a couple apostatises, the marriage shall be judicially dissolved by a divorce. But according to the view of other jurists, such a marriage is to be dissolved without a divorce."[9]

## Application in the modern world

Many countries with majority Muslim populations have implemented Islamic Law, or Shariah, to varying degrees in the modern world. Some countries have proclaimed the Shariah as the overriding basis of their legal systems.

Other countries have made Islam the official religion, but implementation of the Shariah has been restricted to specific areas.[10]

Those countries which have been most forthright in basing their legal codes on Islamic law, and therefore taken action against apostasy, include Pakistan, Saudi Arabia, Mauritania, the Sudan and Iran. The latter, though Shi'i and therefore drawing on different Hadith collections and legal codes, nevertheless takes a similar view to apostasy from Islam to that discussed above. Other countries which draw on Shariah to a lesser degree include Malaysia, which nevertheless has passed legislation prohibiting non-Muslims from attempting to convert a Muslim (though allowing and, indeed, giving official sanction to the reverse).

In the above context of Shariah prohibitions against apostasy, those Muslims who have renounced their faith in countries which follow Islamic Law have often undergone great suffering, discrimination, and persecution.[11]

In Pakistan, human rights agencies have documented many cases where converts away from Islam have been targeted by local Islamic and civil authorities. The case of Tahir Iqbal serves as an example. After converting from Islam to Christianity in 1988, Iqbal was accused by local Islamic leaders of defiling a copy of the Qur'an. He was arrested, and imprisoned for over 18 months. Repeated requests

---

[9] Al-Qayrawani, "The Risala: A Treatise on Maliki Fiqh". Section 32.11 Effects Of Change Of Religion.

[10] Cf. Pew Research Center, "The World's Muslims: Religion, Politics and Society," 2013, accessed 16 May, 2017, http://www.pewforum.org/2013/04/30/the-worlds-muslims-religion-politics-society-overview/.

[11] According to the *Freedom of Thought Report 2015* (http://freethoughtreport.com/), the following countries prescribe death as the punishment for apostasy. All relate to Muslim-majority communities: Somalia, Sudan, Mauritania, Nigeria (Islamist controlled areas), Brunei Darussalam, Malaysia (certain states), Afghanistan, Pakistan (blasphemy), Iran, Maldives, Iraq, Qatar, Saudi Arabia, United Arab Emirates, Yemen.

for bail by his counsel were refused, and he was found dead in his cell amid suspicious circumstances in July 1992.[12] The more recent case of Asia Bibi, a Pakistani Christian woman who has languished in prison for years on trumped up charges of blasphemy highlights the scandal of these laws and the extent of their abuse in Pakistan.[13]

Cases of harassment, discrimination or persecution of converts have also been documented by human rights or church groups in Egypt, Morocco, Somalia, Sudan, Saudi Arabia and Iran. In the latter country, a number of pastors actively involved in evangelising Muslims have been murdered in recent decades, with complicity by local government and Islamic authorities strongly suspected by church groups.

Muslims living in the West can also face difficulties if they choose to convert to Christianity. Though the threat of death is less prevalent than in Muslim societies, converts in Western countries still often face rejection by their families and communities, disinheritance, and possible divorce if their marital partner does not also convert. Physical intimidation of apostates is increasingly common in Western locations where Muslims have settled in large numbers.[14]

Conversion represents one of the greatest obstacles in Christian-Muslim interaction in the modern world. However, this should not cause it to be swept under the carpet. Indeed, it cries out for sensitive discussion. Western societies are increasingly playing host to Muslim immigrant communities, and Muslim mission activity in the West is increasingly widespread and sophisticated, and is benefiting from freedom of speech and multicultural policies in western countries. At the same time, Muslim majority countries typically impose stringent restrictions on mission activity to

> *Muslim-majority communities are denied the same type of access to multiple faith options as is enjoyed by non-Muslim majorities in Western countries."*

---

[12] Amnesty International, "Pakistan: Use and Abuse of the Blasphemy Laws," July 1994, https://www.amnesty.org/en/documents/asa33/008/1994/en/.

[13] Madeeha Bakhsh, "Trial of blasphemy accused Asia Bibi 'likely' to resume in June," April 21, 2017, accessed 29 July, 2017, https://www.christiansinpakistan.com/trial-of-blasphemy-accused-asia-bibi-likely-to-resume-in-june/.

[14] "The ex-Muslim Britons who are persecuted for being atheists," accessed 16 May, 2017, http://www.bbc.com/news/magazine-34357047.

Muslims by non-Muslim faith adherents. Thus Muslim-majority communities are denied the same type of access to multiple faith options as is enjoyed by non-Muslim majorities in Western countries.

## Dissenting Muslims voices

As signalled above, there are small numbers of prominent Muslims who do not adhere to the standard line of death for apostates. For example, the former leader of the Sudan, Dr Hasan al-Turabi, argued that the scriptural prohibition against apostasy was time-bound, saying:

> "The Prophet, peace be upon him, explained that one who abandons his religion and deserts his fellows should be killed. Regrettably, people of subsequent generations have taken the Prophet's saying out of its historical context and generalised it. In so doing they deny one of the basic truths of Islam: the freedom of faith. How can it be imagined by a rational person that Allah, Who had compelled none to believe, allows us the right to compel others and force them to believe? The Qur'anic verses that prohibit compulsion and coercion are numerous and so are the sayings and practices of the Prophet, peace be upon him. That is why I do not hold the common view on the question of apostasy."[15]

Such views are encouraging but in the early 21$^{st}$ century are representative of a tiny minority of Muslims. Moreover, they have attracted severe condemnation from many Muslim scholars who take a more traditional Islamic view on the question.

## How should Christians respond?

Christians both outside and within the Muslim world can respond to the above situation in various ways:

- They can support human rights groups engaged in advocacy on behalf of Christian minorities experiencing discrimination.

- They can express support through letters to newspapers, politicians etc. for the full implementation in Muslim countries of the Universal Declaration of Human Rights provision relating to religious freedom.

---

[15] Hassan Abdullah Al-Turabi, "Opinion on Apostasy stirs a Heated Debate in Islamic Juristic Circles," *The Diplomat*, no. 2 (Muharram 1417 / June 1996): 39.

- They can bring these issues to the attention of their local churches for action through prayer, support for missions outreach, etc.

- They can sensitively discuss these issues with individual Muslim friends, neighbours, work colleagues etc., urging them to take up such matters with Muslim representative bodies.

- They can encourage their churches to engage in dialogue on these issues with local mosques and Islamic centres.

## What about the anti-reciprocity argument?

Consider the following report, which raises the much-discussed issue of reciprocity. The report is drawn from *Asia Times Online*, and refers to an interview with Abdul Hadi Awang, former Chief Minister of the Malaysian State of Terengganu and President of the conservative Islamic political party, PAS, which governed in Terengganu from 1999-2004:

> "Hadi was asked if it was true that an application to build a new Catholic church in Kuala Terengganu had not yet received a favorable reply. Hadi said the state had studied the matter and found out that the place currently being used was adequate for the church's requirements (Catholics there have been using a chapel belonging to a local convent). "To build a new church, with a tall steeple and *lambang* [symbol or cross], in a public place would be a sensitive issue," he said. "They [the Church] have to consider the sensitivities of the community around them. They have a place of worship now; we think it is adequate. We would allow them to build a *dewan* [hall], but not a prominent steeple. It's for their own safety." When asked why this issue should be "sensitive", Hadi said there were certain quarters, a small minority, in society who were *jahil* (ignorant) and that they could create problems. He also said the state government could not guarantee security against such problems as it does not control the security forces, which come under federal jurisdiction."[16]

Readers familiar with London in the early 21st century might find themselves thinking comparatively of the imposing East London mosque, which broadcasts the Islamic call to prayer throughout that part of London, historically one of the great capitals of the Christian

---

[16] Anil Netto, "Malaysia: PAS Winning Few Hearts so Far," *Asia Times Online*, March 6, 2004, http://www.atimes.com/atimes/Southeast_Asia/FC06Ae04.html.

world. It would seem that majority Christian London is far more open to overt expressions of alternative faith adherence than were the Muslim PAS authorities in the Malaysian state of Terengganu.

Does this case raise issues of reciprocity which call for Christian attention and discussion? It would appear so. Christians involved in dialogue with Muslims need to speak not only for the masses they represent directly in their own countries, but also for the faceless minorities from their faith tradition situated in lands where the Muslim dialogue partner is in the majority, such as in Malaysia. It seems only fair that the efforts extended by Western countries which are home to nominally Christian majorities to provide equal opportunity to Muslim minorities should be reciprocated by Muslim-majority countries vis-à-vis their Christian minorities.

Not all Christians agree with this. The Islam in Europe Committee of the European churches produced a document in February 1997 which rejected the use of the term "reciprocity", arguing that reconciliation was a more desirable goal in pursuing greater Muslim-Christian bridge-building.[17]

In a letter to Dr Ata'ullah Siddiqui of the Islamic Foundation in Leicester simultaneous to the European churches document, Dr Christopher Lamb, former Secretary of the Council of Churches of Britain and Ireland, wrote "we have... decided to reject the whole concept of reciprocity as a basis for Christian/Muslim relationships." Tarek Mitri of the World Council of Churches asserts in a similar vein that "the call for 'reciprocity' in the treatment of minorities is problematic".[18]

Affirming the line taken in the European Churches' document, Muslim authors at the Islamic Foundation in Leicester lamented that:

> "... so often European Christians contrast the allegedly good treatment of Muslims in European countries (apart from Bosnia) with the allegedly bad treatment of Christians in Muslim countries. The way the comparison is made usually suggests that since Muslims treat Christians badly (it is said),

---

[17] *Reciprocity and Beyond: A Muslim Response to the European Churches' Document on Islam*, (Leicester: Islamic Foundation, 1997), 21-23.

[18] Michael Ipgrave (ed.), *The Road Ahead: A Christian–Muslim Dialogue* (London: Church House Publishing, 2002), 107.

then there is no reason for Christians to treat Muslims well or even justly..."[19]

In fact, this statement does not accurately articulate the argument for reciprocity, which clearly calls for advocacy on behalf of Christian minorities in majority-Muslim lands, but certainly does not advocate discrimination against Muslim minorities in majority-Christian lands. Nevertheless, there seems to be a meeting of the minds between such Muslim statements and the views of the anti-reciprocity exponents in the Churches.

While the eloquent argumentation of those Christians who reject the notion of reciprocity may persuade certain Christian scholars and please some Muslim interlocutors, it is hard to ignore an impression of disloyalty and abandonment resulting from Western Christian leaders who refuse to advocate forcefully on behalf of any Christian minority in a Muslim majority location which is experiencing discrimination.

> *Cardinal Francis Arinze: "People of the majority religion in a country should not deny to religious minorities in that country the very freedom of religion that they claim for their coreligionists in another country where they are in the minority."*

In this context, strong affirmation should be given to the views of Roman Catholic Cardinal Francis Arinze, President of the Pontifical Council for Interreligious Dialogue from 1985–2002, who writes as follows:

> "... The right to religious freedom ... applies wherever there is a human being. People of the majority religion in a country should not therefore deny to religious minorities in that country the very freedom of religion that they claim for their coreligionists in another country where they are in the minority. This is what reciprocity is all about. In order to build for peace, we need the acceptance and practice of reciprocity."[20]

---

[19] *Reciprocity and Beyond*, 4-5. The tone of this statement is reiterated in Ataullah Siddiqui, "Issues in Co-existence and Dialogue: Muslims and Christians in Britain," in *Muslim–Christian Perceptions of Dialogue Today: Experiences and Expectations*, ed. Jacques Waardenburg (Leuven: Peeters, 2000), 194-95.

[20] Francis Arinze, *Religions for Peace: A Call for Solidarity to the Religions of the World* (London: Darton, Longman & Todd, 2002), 134.

Similarly, former Archbishop of Canterbury, George Carey, deserves support in making the following forthright statement:

> "During my time as archbishop, this was my constant refrain – that the welcome we have given to Muslims in the West, with the accompanying freedom to worship freely and build their mosques, should be reciprocated in Muslim lands."[21]

Furthermore, an Eastern Orthodox voice would be appropriate at this point, given the daily experience of much of Eastern Orthodoxy under Islamic rule:

> "... greater care should be taken in the future to avoid a new mistake: that in the name of cultivating a good climate for the Muslim-Christian dialogue, the poor and miserable Orthodox minorities who live in Muslim majorities are forgotten or even sacrificed. Parallel to the polite stance and respect for the Muslims who live in the West, similar support is needed for Christians who are oppressed in intolerant Islamic environments in Africa and Asia. The contemporary Muslim-Christian dialogue should take into consideration these international situations that require coexistence and mutual dependence."[22]

---

[21] Jonathan Petre, "Carey's Scathing Assault on Islam," 27 March, 2004, accessed 10 June, 2005, http://smh.com.au.

[22] Anastasios Yannoulatos, "Byzantine and Contemporary Greek Orthodox Approaches to Islam'," *Journal of Ecumenical Studies* 33, no. 4 (Fall 1996): 525.

# Religion, Society and the Public Discourse

## Is religion now back on the public agenda in the West?

Samuel Huntington's Clash of Civilisations theory[1] may well have gathered cobwebs along with countless other scholarly theories if it had not been for the 9/11 attacks. That event gave the Huntington theory a new lease of life, and represented a watershed moment in the revival of interest in and discussion about religion in the West.

The tragedy of 9/11, plus the many ensuing terrorist attacks around the world, the campaigns of Islamic State and other events, have given new impetus to flagging efforts to bridge Christian-Muslim divides. There has been a surge in Christian-Muslim engagement at all levels: political leadership, religious leadership as well as grassroots structures among Christians and Muslims.

> *The 9/11 attacks were a watershed moment in the revival of interest in and discussion about religion in the West.*

The attacks of September 11, 2001 have, in that way, had a positive effect, though this is offset by the fact that the West-Islam tension is worse than it has been for perhaps 100 years.

In sum, religion is now a hot topic, especially where the Christian-Muslim interface is concerned. For those who work as Christian specialists in the study of Islam, describing their work is no longer a conversation stopper in social gatherings; quite the reverse.

Nevertheless, some faces of Christianity are seen as more palatable by officialdom in the current climate than others. The movement towards greater Christian-Muslim bridge-building means that the favour of Government officialdom falls on those sections of Christianity inclined to the dialogue paradigm, more than traditional mission or more robust methods of exchange. In other words,

---

[1] "...the fundamental source of conflict in this new world will not be primarily ideological or primarily economic. The great divisions among humankind and the dominating source of conflict will be cultural." Samuel P. Huntington, "The Clash of Civilizations?," *Foreign Affairs* 72 (1993):22. See also Samuel P. Huntington, *The Clash of Civilizations and the Remaking of World Order* (New York: Simon & Schuster, 1996).

Christianity is now more on the public agenda in the West, but it is a particular face of Christianity which has benefited in the current climate.

Some commentators argue that evangelicalism has not been the beneficiary of the newfound interest in religious affairs. For example, Giles Fraser, Anglican Vicar of St Mary's, Newington, and left-leaning journalist and commentator in British broadsheets, asserts that "the word evangelical is now firmly linked in the public imagination with intolerance and bigotry."[2]

However, such statements seem to conflate "the public imagination" with the perspective of the author. They stand in contrast to the widely-reported growth in evangelicalism within mainline denominations, such as the Anglican Church, at the expense of more liberal elements within the Church.[3]

In this context, as religion works its way more overtly into public discourse, we can expect to see a more visible presence of issues dear to evangelicals, such as religious liberty as well as mission and evangelism.

### How should Christians respond to the push for Shariah Law in Western countries?

Today there is an increasing push for acceptance of aspects of Shariah law in both the Muslim world and the West.[4] A core goal of the Islamic State of Iraq and Syria was to establish Shariah law in the regions that they controlled after 2014; this was also the case with the Taliban during their years of rule in Afghanistan from 1996 to 2001. So it is important to be clear on just what Shariah is.

The concept appears obliquely in the Qur'an at verse 45:18: "*Then We put thee on the (right) Way of Religion [Shariah]: so follow thou that (Way), and follow not the desires of those who know not*". This gives support to the common Muslim view that Shariah law is divinely

---

[2] Giles Fraser, "Evangelicals Have Become This Century's Witch Burners," *The Guardian* 14 July, 2003.

[3] "The Church of England: Resurrection?," *The Economist,* January 9, 2016, http://www.economist.com/news/britain/21685473-parts-established-church-are-learning-their-immigrant-brethren-resurrection.

[4] Patricia Sloane-White, *Corporate Islam: Sharia and the modern workplace* (New York: Cambridge University Press, 2017).

sourced and fixed, and is a gift to humanity from Allah to guide Muslims on how to live and govern correctly.

Several different schools of legal interpretation emerged within 200 years of the death of Muhammad in 632. Of these, four survived among majority Sunni Muslims: the Hanafite, Malikite, Shafi'ite, and Hanbalite schools, the last being the most conservative/literalist.

Shariah legal codes are marked with **inequality**. Four example, in Shariah courts "all jurists, court officials and the judge must be Muslims; non-Muslims are not allowed to take part in any way. No woman may become a judge".[5]

For aspects of family law, Shariah law codes draw on the Qur'an (verses 2-3 of chapter 4) to permit polygamy. But Choice is not equal across the genders. A Muslim male can marry Jewish or Christian women, but a Muslim female must marry a Muslim male. This reflects the view that the identity of families is determined by the religious identity of the father.

The institution of divorce is similarly weighted towards male advantage. Islamic law understands the husband to be the divorcer; "there is consensus that the divorcee is the wife".[6] In cases of divorce, mothers can lose custody of children after the age of seven. And when both parents died, sons stand to inherit twice as much as daughters according to the dictates of Shariah Law.

So in mixed marriages where the wife is Jewish or Christian, she stands to lose heavily if the marriage fails, as the children are considered Muslim and therefore the custody remains with the father. If a Muslim converts to another faith, he/she loses all rights to custody of children and inheritance, "except if he returns and repents before the distribution of the heritage".[7]

In the courtroom, testimony is weighted in favour of Muslim males over Muslim females, and more generally of Muslims over non-Muslims. In each case, the testimony of the former carries twice the weighting of the latter. Furthermore, "In rape cases only a Muslim male witness' evidence is admissible".[8]

---

[5] S. Solomon and K. Wakeling, *A Comparison Table of Shari'ah Law and English Law*, (London: Christian Concern for our Nation, 2009), 9.

[6] M.J. Maghniyyah, *The Five Schools of Islamic Law: Al-Hanafi, al-Hanbali, al-Ja'fari, al-Maliki, al-Shafi'i*, (Qum, Iran: Ansariyan, 1995), 383.

[7] Maghniyyah, *The Five Schools of Islamic Law*, 468.

[8] Solomon & Wakeling, *A Comparison Table*, 12

Not only is Shariah Law unequal in its implementation, but it also tends to be **excessive**. The application of the hudud criminal codes clearly shows excess, with public floggings, amputation of limbs, and execution by stoning stipulated for various crimes.

> *If some Muslim insiders stand against Islamic law, non-Muslims should be sceptical when being presented with sugar-coated versions of Shariah.*

Many ordinary Muslims have a highly negative view of the Islamic legal codes, and migrated to the West to get away from Shariah law. If some Muslim insiders stand against Islamic law, non-Muslims should be sceptical when being presented with sugar-coated versions of Shariah. This is happening increasingly in Western countries, with some Muslim activist groups pushing for parallel systems in family law to allow for Shariah tribunals, and making a concerted push for the adaptation of aspects of Shariah Finance in Western financial institutions such as banks.

## How should Christians respond to a mosque being built in their neighbourhood?

This particular issue has been a source of some considerable debate throughout the West for many decades, with the increased presence of non-Christian faiths in Western countries. Numbers of mosques have increased rapidly across Western countries; the following table captures well the sense of dramatic growth of Muslim houses of worship:

| Country | First mosque | Growth in mosques (in recent years) |
|---|---|---|
| UK | 1891 | 4 (1960) –> 314 (1985) –> 618 (2002)[9] |
| Australia | 1882 | 340[10] |

---

[9] Peter Brierley, "Muslim Growth in the United Kingdom and Worldwide," accessed 17 May, 2017, https://www.lausanneworldpulse.com/research-php/654/03-2007.

[10] Sam Bowker, "The Australian Mosque," accessed 17 May, 2017, http://www.abc.net.au/news/2016-09-23/the-australian-mosque/7868256.

| New Zealand | 1959 | 42[11] |
| USA | 1929 | 1209 to 2106 (2000-2010)[12] |
| France | 1926 | 2500[13] |
| Germany | 1924 | 3 -> 159 (1990-2008)[14] |

This rapid expansion in mosque construction triggered concern among many people in Western countries, as reflected in the following question submitted for discussion at a public lecture in Britain in 2002: "How do we stop small Islamic towns spreading in our own country? Certain areas have Islamic councils, schools, Muslim enclaves etc. Shouldn't we be just as concerned about the situation in our own backyard as we are in international events?"

This raises challenging questions, because it relates to the identity of ordinary neighbourhoods. But whether the issue is the construction of a mosque, or of a house of worship of a faith other than our own, or indeed the construction of some landmark which is going to alter the existing identity of the community in some way, it is a fact that people feel threatened.

Western communities are no different from other societies in wishing to preserve intact a perceived long-held identity. Furthermore, and in this context, it is natural for Christians to feel uncomfortable when mosques are created among existing communities for the first time.

At the same that time, no society is static; societies evolve in myriad ways. Neighbourhoods change in their make-up; no community can be frozen in time and form. Western societies based on Judeo-Christian and democratic values and principles cannot accept a system which says that only one type of citizen will live in a certain neighbourhood and a different type of citizen will not. This would be tantamount to apartheid.

---

[11] "Mosques and Islamic Schools in New Zealand," accessed 18 May, 2017, https://www.salatomatic.com/reg/New-Zealand/uJt2QgpcxO.

[12] "List of mosques in the United States," accessed 17 May, 2017, https://en.wikipedia.org/wiki/List_of_mosques_in_the_United_States.

[13] Yasmeen Serhan, "France's Disappearing Mosques," accessed 17 May, 2017, https://www.theatlantic.com/news/archive/2016/08/french-mosques-islam/493919/.

[14] "Germany approves huge mosque construction," accessed 17 May, 2017, http://www.middle-east-online.com/english/?id=27616.

There will always be movement of populations, and people who make such moves, regardless of ethnicity, creed or culture, want to bring the symbols of their faith with them. So, if Muslims move in increasing numbers to a particular neighbourhood, they will want to establish a mosque. In a free society adherents of different faiths should have the right to set up their own places of worship.

> *It is important that immigrant communities show sensitivity in the way they establish the symbols of their faith within a community for the first time.*

At the same time, it is important that immigrant communities show sensitivity in the way they establish the symbols of their faith within a community for the first time. For example, it would not be tactful for the very first mosque erected in a town to dominate the skyline. Local councils in Western countries should design new or implement existing planning guidelines[15] which ensure that houses of worship of a faith previously not represented in a town or neighbourhood are constructed in such a way as to blend in with, rather than dominate, an existing community.

A clear example of how insensitive actions by minority groups can arouse hostility from a majority community which feels its identity is being threatened surrounded a case in the central Italian town of L'Aquila in October 2003. A Muslim rights advocate launched a court case in which he called for the removal of crucifixes from the state primary school his children attended. The judge, in ruling in favour of the Muslim complainant, stated that "The presence of the symbol of the cross shows the will of the state to put Catholicism at the centre of the universe as the absolute truth."[16] The ruling drew a strong response from some Catholic Church figures, with Cardinal Ersilio Tonini stating that "You cannot remove a symbol of the

---

[15] Such guidelines exist in many areas of Britain. However, an often-heard complaint from Christians is that minority immigrant communities find it far easier to gain approvals for building projects than do white majority communities, because local councils are reluctant to attract accusations of racism by refusing applications from the minority groups.

[16] Sophie Arie, "Muslim Wins Italian Court Ban on Crucifixes in Classroom," *The Guardian* 27 October, 2003.

religious and cultural values of a people just because it can offend someone."[17]

Furthermore, immigrant communities should not themselves practice a kind of apartheid. Towns should not be permitted to become largely Muslim ghettos, as has occurred with many towns in the north of England due to the British Government's hands-off policy of multiculturalism over several decades. Interaction between communities is important; faith communities need to mix together in order to build an atmosphere of understanding and tolerance, reflecting the increasingly multi-religious nature of Western societies.

In order for this to happen, both national and local governing authorities should explore appropriate means of intervention and community engineering, such as the Australian Department of Immigration's regional migration programs that have sought to encourage migrants to settle in country towns rather than large cities.[18] Christians can lobby their members of parliament in favour of this kind of government intervention.

### Is the term "multi-faith" appropriate for Western countries?

One question I was asked at a public lecture in London some years ago was as follows: "Bearing in mind the 71:6 percentage Christian: Other Faiths split in Britain, is not the use of the word 'multi-faith' – implying an equal spread – unfortunate, leading to a case of the tail wagging the dog in the formulation of national policies?"[19]

If the term "multi-faith" is used in a descriptive fashion to reflect the fact that multiple faiths are represented in Western countries, it is entirely appropriate for the early 21$^{st}$ century. Indeed, this usage would have been appropriate for virtually any period of past history in the case of Britain, for example, as there has never been a time that Britain has only had one single religious faith represented among its citizens.

However, the above question implies another dimension; namely that faiths representing a relatively small minority of Western

---

[17] "Storm over Italy crucifix ruling," 26 October, 2003, accessed 29 July, 2017, http://news.bbc.co.uk/1/hi/world/europe/3215445.stm.

[18] "Rural Australia attracting immigrants," accessed 17 May, 2017, http://www.workpermit.com/news/rural-australia-attracting-immigrants-20060130.

[19] Since the question was asked in 2002, Britain's religious demography has continued to change rapidly. The 2011 National Census revealed a different ratio of 59:9 for Christians: Other Faiths.

populations have come to exercise a disproportionate amount of influence in the formulation of government policy regarding faith matters. This impression can easily be gained by a perusal of the BBC Religion and Ethics website,[20] where different faiths are given equal space, without any suggestion of proportional differences among the population at large.

Such is the fruit of multicultural policies which have become increasingly uncomfortable using terms such as "majority" and "minority", preferring instead to view society as a mosaic where the size of the disparate elements is immaterial or should be deliberately ignored.

## Should Christians embrace the People of Faith notion?

A certain phenomenon has gained widespread currency in inter-faith circles. This phenomenon, which we might term the "People of Faith" notion, argues that there should be a substantial measure of common identification in the West between people of different faiths who actively practice their faith. The proponents of this view see this group as distinct from the broad masses of Western societies who are either nominal adherents of a faith (mostly Christianity) but do not practice it on a regular basis, or regularly declare themselves to have no faith in national censuses (25.7% in the UK in 2011; 22.3% in Australia in 2011; 38.5% in New Zealand in 2013).

Christians need to consider with caution the ramifications of this People of Faith notion. It is based on the implicit argument that those citizens who practice Christianity should identify themselves first and foremost, not with a significant percentage of Western populations who also express some allegiance to Christianity, but rather with observant Muslims, Hindus, Buddhists, Sikhs, Jews and so forth.

This has considerable significance for access to the corridors of power enjoyed by Christians. In Britain, for example, the Head of State, the Queen, is also the Head of the (Anglican) Church of England and the (Presbyterian) Church of Scotland. There are presently 21 Anglican Bishops who sit in the House of Lords. State funding is available to vast numbers of Christian schools (though also in lesser measure to

---

[20] "BBC Religion & Ethics," accessed 17 May, 2017, http://www.bbc.co.uk/religion. The religions allocated space are Atheism, Bahá'í, Buddhism, Christianity, Hinduism, Islam, Judaism, Mormonism, Paganism, Sikhism.

Jewish and Muslim schools). There are many other ways that Christianity sits in a privileged position among the faiths in Britain.

Arguments in favour of the status quo can be articulated (though not without challenge) if Christianity is seen in clear terms as being the faith of the majority. If, however, practising Christians present their faith as representing a small minority of the populations of Western countries such as Britain, Australia and New Zealand, reflecting the situation of other faiths in these countries, then the advantages enjoyed by Christianity as a majority faith will be unsustainable in the short to medium term.

In Britain, for example, the outcome is likely to be either disestablishment of the Church of England or an adjustment of the status quo so that the instruments of power and influence currently wielded by Christians, especially by the Church of England, are shared with other faiths present in Britain. This latter scenario has been called for by some representatives of other faiths, especially by Muslims.

In other Western countries where Christianity is not the established faith, such as in Australia and New Zealand, nevertheless the fact that a considerable majority of citizens opt to identify themselves as Christian provides to the Christian faith a greater public profile and access to the public square than is enjoyed by other religions which claim a much smaller following (e.g. Islam: 2.2% in Australia; 1% in New Zealand). In this context, practicing Christians should embrace their less-active co-religionists rather than shunning them in favour of an embrace with practicing Muslims, Hindus, Buddhists and others.

Furthermore, a sub-category of the "People of Faith" notion has made an appearance on the multi-faith stage; namely the "Abrahamic Faiths" category. There is an increasing tendency to lump together Jews, Christians, and Muslims in this category, drawing attention to a common link with Abraham and, in the case of Christians and Muslims, common figures like Jesus.

British theologian Dr Toby Howarth engages with this view in the following terms:

> "Some Christians warmly embrace this idea of kinship between the three religions, taking it as the starting–point of their relationship, while others reject out of hand the idea that Muslims might be their religious 'cousins'. But whatever their

feelings, Christians need to take seriously the Muslim *claim* to Abrahamic religious descent. They also need to acknowledge the clear kinship of *religious ideas* that binds Christianity with Islam and Judaism, and distinguishes these three from other great world religions such as Buddhism and Hinduism."[21]

However, this approach potentially provides support for a view of Muslim supersessionism (or replacement theology)[22], with the Islamic doctrine of People of the Book allowing Muslims to say "yes, of course we accept you Jews and Christians ... all you need to do is accept Muhammad, the seal of the prophets, and the Qur'an". Accepting the prophet of Islam and the Qur'an in this way would be tantamount to accepting Islam, given the faith's claim to supersede Judaism and Christianity. Here is another reason that the "People of Faith" notion needs to be closely scrutinised by Christians and not swallowed wholesale.

In summary, Christians need to think carefully through these issues, so that future scenarios will reflect the understanding and will of the church, rather than Christians realising after the event that decisions have been taken for them.

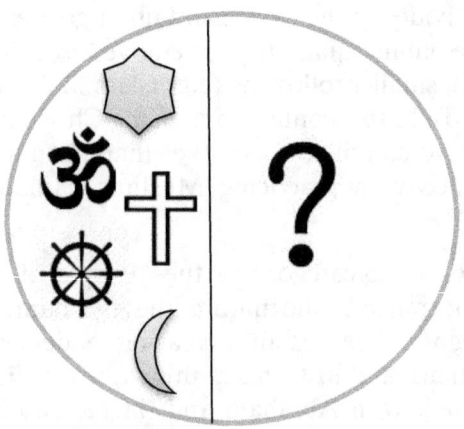

---

[21] Toby Howarth, "9/11: A Call to Integrity in Mission," CMS Annual Sermon 2002, (London: Church Missionary Society, 2002), 5.

[22] A common view among Muslims, where Islam is seen as superseding or replacing Judaism and Christianity.

## *What is the future of multi-faith Western societies?*

In his 2003 volume *The Challenge of Islam to Christians*, the Reverend David Pawson prophesied that Britain would be an Islamic society by the middle of the 21$^{st}$ century.[23] Discussion of such a scenario in various organs of the print and electronic media has become increasingly prominent in the early years of the 21$^{st}$ century. In one particularly well-argued piece, Peter Hitchens reports on a case of a white British non-Muslim family living in a predominantly Muslim neighbourhood in a British city. The two daughters of the family, aged 12 and 9, elected to wear Muslim headcover and attend mosque worship and Qur'an instruction, reflecting practice among their local peer group. Hitchens suggests that this case may well be a window into the future of Britain, where social and moral decay make a religious revival ultimately inevitable, but where Christianity is no longer the leading candidate to lead such a revival.[24]

Some see such views as driven by a sense of alarmism, as well as by a failure to see Muslims in their diversity. Nevertheless, there clearly is a debate to be had on this topic, and such a debate should be aired freely, rather than being muzzled with those articulating views such as the above being shamed into silence. It is a legitimate and necessary exercise to discuss the future of multi-faith Western societies such as Britain and France. Moreover, it is appropriate that we should make a comment on this debate at this point of the present study.

As for the short-term future, it is likely that multi-faith Western nations with rapidly growing Muslim minority communities such as Britain, France and Germany will see a number of changes of a relatively minor nature, but the macro picture will probably not alter substantially. In the middle of the 21$^{st}$ century, the largest faith in such nations will still be Christian, in terms of a very broad definition of Christianity, though it will probably no longer represent more than 50% of the population. The minority faith communities will grow somewhat, including the Islamic community, but not to the point of becoming a majority faith.

---

[23] David Pawson, *The Challenge of Islam to Christians* (London: Hodder & Stoughton, 2003).

[24] Peter Hitchens, "Will Britain Convert to Islam?," *The Mail on Sunday,* 2 November, 2003, http://www.femail.com/pages/standard/article.html?in_page_id=2&in_article_id=201325.

Reports of conversions to Islam tend to capture media interest. Dani Garavelli wrote as follows in 2002, shortly after the 9/11 attacks:

> "About 20,000 British people have converted during the last decade. At Edinburgh's central mosque, there have been 80 "reverts" – Muslims believe that everyone is born into Islam – over the last four years."[25]

Individual testimonies of conversion are frequent in Western media outlets, such as the 2014 story of Lydia who renounced her antipathy towards Islam in favour of embracing the faith in Sydney.[26]

The British Muslim writer Yahya Birt[27] disputes what he sees as exaggerated claims of rates of conversion to Islam, declaring:

> "The first myth to be exploded was the claim that Islam is Britain's second largest (and it is asserted fastest-growing) religion. But this growth has everything to do with immigration and birth rates rather than conversion... out of all the minority religions and the main Christian denominations, Islam is the religion people are least likely to leave or convert to... In other words, it is the least attractive to others and yet paradoxically the most resilient... In the marketplace of faiths, Islam would not appear to be offering an attractive prospect."[28]

In fact, there are many more conversions to Buddhism taking place in Western countries than conversions to Islam. Of the total number of Buddhists in Britain, 50% are converts,[29] and this is likely the case in other Western countries as well. Buddhism carries with it a new age appeal in a pluralistic culture. It is likely that Buddhism will rise significantly in its proportion of faith adherence across the West.

The longer-term future for the West is more difficult to predict, given the unpredictable range of factors and variables involved. But key ingredients for Western countries shoring up their Judeo-Christian heritage for the long term, and disproving the scenario advanced by David Pawson and Peter Hitchens above, will be:

---

[25] Dani Garavelli, "The Attraction of the Veil," *The Times* 10 March, 2002.

[26] "Real life: Australian woman Lydia on why she converted to Islam," accessed 19 May, 2017, http://www.news.com.au/lifestyle/real-life/real-life-australian-woman-lydia-on-why-she-converted-to-islam/news-story/560bf829839cffc6b5ea6085f4a5e672.

[27] Himself a convert to Islam.

[28] Yahya Birt, "Lies! Damn Lies! Statistics and Conversions," *Q-News*, no. 350 (October 2003): 20.

[29] Ibid.

- The churches' ability to strike a balance between loyalty to revealed truth and remaining relevant to social context.

- The churches' commitment to reaching out to vast numbers of nominal Christians in the British population.

- The churches minimising intra-Christian rivalries and disputes;

- Christians getting involved in the public arena through political activity, media involvement, and social advocacy.

- Western nations rediscovering confidence in past identity and achievement, rather than being weighed down by guilt burdens for colonial history.

- Social, ethnic and religious change resulting from immigration being kept at a controlled rate so that majority communities feels that their overall identity is not under threat.[30]

---

[30] For a detailed discussion of this issue, cf. Myles Harris, *Tomorrow is Another Country* (London: Civitas, 2003).

# Where does Spiritual Warfare come into Christian-Muslim Relations?

> *For we wrestle not against flesh and blood, but against principalities, against powers, against the rulers of the darkness of this world...*
> *(Ephesians 6:12)*

How are Christians to interpret such a verse regarding attitudes to other faiths? Two risks present themselves. The first simply ignores such a verse as irrelevant. The second risk, in contrast, too readily applies such a verse to the world around. Neither of these approaches is satisfactory.

## The too-liberal approach

The first risk typically derives from an uncritical acceptance of other faiths as equally valid variations on a divine theme. This is a product of our postmodern context, where subtle but powerful pressures are at work among Western populations on a daily basis to accept all forms of diversity without question. Thus approaches which are most "kosher" in terms of current received wisdom are those which are multi-faith, multi-ethnic, multi-cultural, multi-sexual and so forth.

Furthermore, the first risk represents a kind of lazy thinking. It ignores certain phenomena found in other faiths which seem to derive from forces for evil. A clear example is the radical fundamentalist phenomenon within Islam, which plans and rejoices at terrorist attacks such as those carried out in New York and Washington on September 11, 2001 and which produces thousands of young recruits ready to fight for Islamic State with its practice of murder, beheadings and enslavement.

For example, there is something very dark about the following excerpt of a recorded conversation between Osama Bin Laden and two of his colleagues shortly after the 9/11 attacks:

> *Bin Laden*: After a little while, they announced that another plane had hit the World Trade Center. The brothers who heard the news were overjoyed by it.
>
> *Shaykh*: ... we stayed until four o'clock, listening to the news every time a little bit different, everyone was very joyous and saying "Allah is great," "Allah is great," "We are thankful to

Allah," "Praise Allah." And I was happy for the happiness of my brothers. That day the congratulations were coming on the phone non-stop. The mother was receiving phone calls continuously.

*Shaykh*: Fight them, Allah will torture them, with your hands, he will torture them. He will deceive them and he will give you victory. Allah will forgive the believers, he is knowledgeable about everything.[1]

## The too-literal approach

The second risk is equally unsatisfactory, but for different reasons. It leads to a knee-jerk dismissal of other faiths as lost in every way, often extending to a view of other faiths as instruments of Satan *per se*.[2]

This attitude ignores the fact that adherents of other faiths are commonly driven by a sincere desire to seek, know and please God. Christians might disagree with them about the extent to which Christians and Muslims respectively find God. However, to dismiss them automatically as being on the path of "the rulers of the darkness of this world" seems to be taking issues of disagreement too far.

Such an attitude similarly represents a kind of lazy thinking. It avoids us having to think about the degree to which elements of truth may be found in other faiths. To do so might make us feel vulnerable. However, Christians should have sufficient confidence in our own faith to be prepared to be a little vulnerable in the challenges they tackle.

## Reflections

Let us ground such comments in a live case study. It concerns my Indonesian friend Zayn ud-Din. He was brought up a Muslim and was imbued with the values of his faith by observant parents. He was the eldest of nine children in a poor Javanese family. At 21 he set out for Australia in search of work to assist with the support of his family. We met as he began his journey.

Over a period of 30 years Zayn ud-Din became perhaps the most faithful friend I have ever had. He was devoted to my parents, who

---

[1] "Transcript of Osama bin Laden videotape," December 13, 2001, accessed 2 June, 2015, http://www.cnn.com/2001/US/12/13/tape.transcript.

[2] Cf. Colin Chapman, "Going Soft on Islam?," *Vox Evangelica* XIX (1989): 15-18.

helped him when he was struggling on arrival in Australia. He is a dedicated son, brother, husband and father to his own family.

Zayn ud-Din's name means "The beauty of the Faith". He has always exhibited a quiet faith. He prays at home. He attends mosque on significant occasions. He never attempts to proselytise. He finds great sustenance in his faith in times of trouble and sorrow.

Zayn ud-Din is not under the control of "powers and principalities". Like many other ordinary Muslims, he manifests most, perhaps all, of the qualities called for by the apostle Peter: goodness, knowledge, self-control, perseverance, godliness, brotherly kindness, love.[3]

Christians should recognise that adherents of other faiths are also in quest of God.[4] At the same time, we should be prepared to ask hard questions of other faiths, and have hard questions asked of Christianity in return. In short, Christians should be willing to live with difference. This is far better than either seeking a trite compromise formula based on the lowest common denominator of all faiths, or automatically dismissing adherents of other faiths as being controlled by "the rulers of the darkness of this world."

> *Christians should be prepared to ask hard questions of other faiths, and have hard questions asked of Christianity in return.*

---

[3] 2 Peter 1:5-7.

[4] This does not mean, however, that Christians must believe that other faiths necessarily realise their quest.

# *Evaluating Islam*

Preceding discussion has addressed some of the most thorny issues to do with Christian-Muslim relations. Sensitive areas have been touched upon, and explorations of both Christian and Muslim communities have revealed both positive and negative features. This inevitably leads to questions such as the following, which I received at one public lecture: "How can we evaluate Islam, Muhammad and the Qur'an?" We will answer it by addressing several related and often asked questions.

## *Is Islam a religion of peace?*

A question posed during one of my public lectures has often recurred in other such events: "Can you comment on statements made by politicians and the media that Islam is a religion of Peace? What in the Qur'an/Shariah Law condones or allows the behaviour of radical Islam?" A variation on this question is the following: "In the Qur'an does Allah call for war? If yes, under what circumstances?"

It is true that since 9/11, Muslim moderates and many non-Muslim political spokespeople have repeated on numerous occasions that Islam is a religion of peace. For example, British Foreign Office Minister Mike O'Brian expressed the official view of the British Government in the wake of 9/11 in saying:

> "Islam is a religion of peace. The vast majority of Muslims deplore violence and terrorism and condemned the events of 11 September... I intend to talk about that minority on the fringes who adopt a distorted view of Islam. A minority that is violent and is a threat to Islam and to the rest of the world."[1]

President Obama was an enthusiastic proponent of associating Islam with peace, commenting as follows in a speech in Baltimore in February 2016:

> "For more than a thousand years, people have been drawn to Islam's message of peace. And the very word itself, Islam, comes from *salam* – peace. The standard greeting is *as-salamu alaykum* – peace be upon you. And like so many faiths, Islam is

---

[1] Mike O'Brien, "The Threat of the Modern Kharijites" paper presented at the conference 'Militant Islam in Asia: The Challenges', (Royal United Service Institute for Defence Studies: London, 21 November 2002).

rooted in a commitment to compassion and mercy and justice and charity. Whoever wants to enter paradise, the Prophet Muhammad taught, 'let him treat people the way he would love to be treated.'"[2]

At the same time, radical Islamists have issued statements calling for violence and jihad in certain context, usually quoting Islamic scriptural reference in support of their calls. This can be confusing for non-Muslim observers, who hear two such clearly opposing viewpoints. And both views are regularly expressed by Muslims who draw on the same scriptures in support of their positions.

> *The Islamic sacred texts offer the potential for being interpreted in both a peaceful and a militarist way. It depends on how individual Muslims wish to read them.*

In fact, the answer lies not in an either/or response, but rather in a "both...and" response. The Islamic sacred texts offer the potential for being interpreted in both a peaceful and a militarist way. It depends on how individual Muslims wish to read them.

On the BBC Radio programme "Thought for the Day" on September 13, 2001, Dr Zaki Badawi rejected the actions of the 9/11 terrorist by citing Qur'an 5:32:

> *"We ordained that if anyone killed a person... not in retaliation of murder or in punishment... it would be as if he killed all Mankind. And if anyone saved a life it would be as if he saved the life of all Mankind."*

Muslim moderates would wish to affirm Dr Badawi's use of this verse to condemn violence and killing. It seems unambiguous.

But if one continues to the immediately following verse, the message is significantly different. Qur'an 5:33 is as follows:

> *"The punishment of those who wage war against Allah and His Messenger, and strive with might and main for mischief through the land is: execution, or crucifixion, or the cutting off of hands and feet from opposite sides, or exile from the land: that is their disgrace in this world, and a heavy punishment is theirs in the Hereafter."*

---

[2] "Remarks by the President at Islamic Society of Baltimore," The White House, Office of the Press Secretary, February 03, 2016, accessed 22 May, 2017,
https://obamawhitehouse.archives.gov/the-press-office/2016/02/03/remarks-president-islamic-society-baltimore.

Thus, while Dr Badawi chose to emphasise a more compassionate interpretation of these verses, someone inclined to a more literalist reading of the Islamic scriptures could easily emphasise verse 33 which talks of execution, crucifixion and the cutting off hands and feet.

In this way, one mindset, that of the Muslim moderates, takes a subtle and reason-based approach to the Islamic sacred texts, reading them in the light of the modern world and adapting them accordingly. Radicals, on the other hand, read the texts in a literalist way, focusing on the surface meaning. For them, the specific struggles such as Palestine, Iraq and Chechnya are not even what is at issue; rather it is that they read their Islamic texts to call for non-Muslim infidels to be fought, regardless of the cause.

In effect, there is a titanic struggle taking place between moderates and radicals for the hearts and minds of the Muslim masses in the middle.

**One text, two messages**

## Is terrorism more likely to flow out of Islam than Christianity?

Terrorism is more likely to flow out of Islam than Christianity, for the simple reason that the Islamic sacred texts lend themselves more easily to justifying violence if they are read in a certain way.

While there is no shortage of passages referring to violence and war in the Old Testament, the direction of progressive revelation in the Christian Scriptural canon is clear. It is next to impossible to find scriptural justification from Jesus' statements in the New Testament for hijacking and flying airliners into crowded buildings or for beheading people and running sex-slave markets. However, the 9/11 hijackers and the various radical Islamist groups around the world who praised them, as well as latest violent radical groups such as Islamic State, grounded their statements in abundant verse references from the Qur'an and Hadith, where there is no similarly clear progression from a message encompassing war to one encompassing peace.[3]

> *Muslim moderates need to tackle the verses used by radicals to justify violence and recognize that it is time for some Hadith materials to be downgraded in importance and, indeed, certain Qur'an verses be questioned in terms of their relevance for today.*

Of course, more moderate Muslim voices reject these radical readings of the verses concerned, as seen above. They reinterpret them in their assertions that Islam is a religion of peace. That is helpful, but needs to be taken further – as moderate re-interpretations will not stop radicals reading the same verses to justify violence. Muslim moderates rather need to tackle the verses used by radicals to justify violence – especially where the Hadith collections are concerned – and recognize that it is time for some of the Hadith materials to be downgraded in importance and, indeed, certain Qur'an verses be questioned in terms of their relevance for today. Some moderate Muslims have suggested this, but it hasn't caught on yet. But it has to be Muslims who do this. Non-Muslims can't do it for them.[4]

## How should Islam be studied?

Adherents of all faiths should have the option of studying other faiths. Moreover, the study should be carried out in a spirit of openness and honest critique where necessary.

---

[3] In fact, many scholars argue that the opposite is the case in the Islamic scriptures, with the earlier Meccan chapters lending themselves more to a message of peace and the later Medinan chapters developing the notion of military jihad. Cf. Kenneth Cragg, *The Call of the Minaret* (Oxford: Oxford University Press, 1956), 72ff.

[4] For a more detailed discussion of this issue, cf. Riddell and Cotterell, *Islam in Context: Past, Present and Future*, 205ff.

A common statement heard by non-Muslim lecturers of Islamic Studies is that in order to learn "authentic" Islam, students need to study with Muslim lecturers. The problem with this view is that often Muslim teachers and lecturers will present a view of Islam that favours their own particular sect or ideological perspective. In such circumstances, non-Muslim lecturers of Islamic Studies in schools and universities may be more likely to give students insights into Islam in all its diversity.

In studying Islam there should be no whitewashing of uncomfortable facts or details, such as is identified in several reports published by the American Textbook Council. These reports evaluated the coverage of Islam and the Middle East in widely adopted history textbooks in American schools. A 2003 report found that:

> "... on controversial subjects, world history textbooks make an effort to circumvent unsavoury facts that might cast Islam past or present in anything but a positive light. Islamic achievements are reported with robust enthusiasm. When any dark side surfaces, textbooks run and hide."[5]

In similar vein, a report from 2008 observed:

> "The contest over textbook content increasingly pits evidence-based scholarship against political partisanship, and the victory of scholarship is far from assured. One stratum of U.S. thought—one that is influential in school publishing today—resists ugly facts about Islam that involve violations of liberal ideals and dangers to international security. To worry about Islamic revivalism or to object to a controlling Islamic 'voice' in the nation's history textbooks, no matter the reason or argument, violates multicultural convention and is thus politically risky. Epithets such as 'Islamophobia' deaden the debate."[6]

This is political correctness at its very worst. These reports further found that unlike the treatment of Islamic and other non-Western history, Western history was subjected to the harshest scrutiny and critique.

Paradoxically, this provides a mirror image of the treatment of Western, Christian and Jewish themes in Saudi Arabian school

---

[5] "Islam and the Textbooks," accessed 30 May, 2017, http://www.meforum.org/559/islam-and-the-textbooks.

[6] Gilbert Sewall, *Islam in the Classroom: What the Textbooks Tell Us* (New York: American Textbook Council, 2008), 47-48.

textbooks, where these themes are often expressed in vitriolic and hateful terms, according to another study.[7]

## If we'd like to understand Islam more should we read the Qur'an for ourselves?

> *Students of Islam should obtain a copy of the Qur'an that is arranged according to the chronological order of its chapters.*

It is certainly helpful for Christians who want to understand more about Islam to read the Qur'an. However, unlike the Bible which is arranged in roughly chronological order according to the dates of the various books, the Qur'an is not arranged chronologically. So non-Muslims who read it from cover to cover will struggle to get a sense of the development of Qur'anic thinking and teaching.

The solution is straightforward. Students of Islam should obtain a copy of the Qur'an that is arranged according to the chronological order of its chapters (*surahs*). Alternatively there are copies online, or such students can follow the order of *surahs* prescribed by Theodor Nöldeke, a German scholar who developed a widely used chronological order of Qur'an surahs.[8]

The point is that the Qur'an in many ways reflects the life and thinking of Muhammad. His thinking evolved over time, so it's important to read the Qur'an chapters in the time order that matches his life progress. That way it is easy to see how some of his attitudes changed over time, such as his views of Jews and Christians, or his teachings on his own role.

## Muslims criticise the Bible and say that it is not reliable and accurate. How reliable and accurate is the Qur'an?

The short answer to this important question is that the usual Muslim claim that the Qur'an has not changed in the slightest way since the

---

[7] Michelle Dardashti, "Survey: Saudi Arabian Textbooks Filled with Hatred of West, Jews'," accessed 10 April, 2004,
http://www.jta.org/page_view_story.asp?intarticleid=12426&intcategoryid=3.

[8] "Theodor Nöldeke," accessed 2 June, 2017,
https://en.wikipedia.org/wiki/Theodor_N%C3%B6ldeke#N.C3.B6ldeke_Chronology.

time of Muhammad cannot be sustained. There is a vast and rapidly expanding body of evidence to that effect. It is highly likely that the Qur'an evolved over time to assume its final form, just as the Bible did.

There is an increasing volume of both scholarly and popular writing about this.[9]

---

[9] For accessible discussion of the important discovery of Qur'an fragments in San'a, Yemen, cf. Toby Lester, "What is the Koran?", *The Atlantic Monthly*, January 1999, https://www.theatlantic.com/magazine/archive/1999/01/what-is-the-koran/304024/; also "The end of the Quran as Muslims know it: Today's Quran in the light of its early manuscripts", *Answering Islam*, http://www.answering-islam.org/authors/oskar/palimpsest.html.

## Truth and Christian-Muslim Relations

"Since the Qur'an declares that "Jesus did not die, it was only made to appear so!", and Muslims are required to declare this and not to discuss it, in what way can there be any hope for reconciliation between the two faiths?"

The essence of this question, posed at the 2003 London Lectures, relates to conflicting truth claims between Christianity and Islam.

One of the characteristic features of post-modernism has been a pervasive sense of coyness in using terms which suggest a value judgement. A substantial body of terminology expressing opposites – right/wrong, good/bad, mainstream/fringe – has

*Western society seems to have advanced in terms of understanding the complexity of the world but has also developed an increasing reluctance to evaluate that complexity.*

been increasingly ruled "out of court". Western society seems to have advanced in terms of understanding the complexity of the world but has also developed an increasing reluctance to evaluate that complexity. It is increasingly unacceptable in postmodern times to state a position or declare an opinion if it is at variance with contemporary received wisdom which says that all things are equal and that positions, attitudes, ideologies and faiths must not be dismissed as wrong or false – rather they should all be seen as equally valid variations on an ideological or godly theme. This situation derives from the postmodern approach to Truth.[1] Truth has come to be seen as internal to the individual, changing, and relative.

A paradox arises from the fact that this contemporary received wisdom on the meaning of truth has assumed a tyranny of its own. It has become the dominant ideology in the early 21st century, like a blanket smothering alternative perspectives. Those who do not swim with the current tide are dismissed as "right-wing" fossils, beyond redemption, rather than being seen as proponents of an equally valid

---
[1] Peter Hicks, *Truth: Could it Be True?* (Carlisle: Solway, 1996), 107.

ideology – which one could reasonably expect in terms of postmodern ideology. Bruce Kaye writes that:

> "... the great danger in postmodernism is that sovereignty will be reconstructed in terms of its caricature tyranny, while on the other hand in the secular mind difference will be so construed that religion has no place at all."[2]

Thus important boundary markers to help us negotiate our way through a complex world have been increasingly denied to us. A resulting sense of disorientation is captured neatly by Middleton and Walsh who paint a portrait of the "Crisis of our Times":

> "It is the kind of chill you feel on the top floor of the tower of modern civilisation ... it is a floor with shattered walls, broken windows and the roof torn off by the postmodern winds of these icy heights ... it feels as if our whole culture has the willies."[3]

How does this relate to Christian-Muslim relations? Muslims are experiencing similar kinds of stresses and irritations with what seems to them as postmodern anarchy. Seyyed Hossein Nasr writes of:

> "... the reassertion at this late hour of human history of tradition which itself is both of a primordial character and possesses continuity over the ages, made possible once again by access to that Truth by which human beings have lived during most – or rather nearly all – of their terrestrial history. This Truth had to be stated anew and reformulated in the name of tradition precisely because of the nearly total eclipse and loss of that reality which has constituted the matrix of life of normal humanity over the ages."[4]

In approaching another great faith, Islam, which has certain exclusivist claims like Christianity and which is experiencing similar stresses in these postmodern times, the challenge for Christians is to find a way to harness this commonality without being forced into adopting the extreme relativism championed by postmodernism.

Muslims are no less concerned with seeking Truth than are Christians. One of the ninety-nine names of Allah in Islam is *al-Haqq* (The Truth), and this underpins much Muslim writing which expresses exclusivist claims about Truth as understood by Islam.

---

[2] Bruce Kaye, "Many Aspects of Pluralism," *St Mark's Review*, no. 171 (Spring 1997): 5.

[3] J. R. Middleton and B. J. Walsh, *Truth is Stranger than it Used to Be: Biblical Faith in a Postmodern Age* (London: SPCK, 1995), 25.

[4] Seyyed Hossein Nasr, *Knowledge and the Sacred* (New York: Crossroad, 1981), 66.

Many Muslims feel a sense of great pain at the degree to which their faith is being eroded by postmodern values in the West.

Christian writers articulate similar concerns. For example, in Green's *The Truth of God Incarnate*, he decries what he sees as the progressive dismemberment of the truth of the Christian faith, saying:

> "How much can you remove from a car, and still possess what is properly called a car? Lights may be a luxury; you can do without bodywork in warm weather; brakes may be dispensed with, at all events on the level; but if you remove the engine or the chassis it is questionable whether we are still talking about a car at all."[5]

In other words, Green feels that the very essence of Christianity has been discarded by many in the Church in order to "move with the postmodern times", as it were. He is responding to some such as a gathering of Anglican clergy of the *Sea of Faith* group who do not

> "believe in the authenticity of the Christmas story, as related in the New Testament, or the resurrection. Instead, [the group] believes that God is a mystical and personal experience which has no physical incarnation."[6]

Green's views of truth is at one with traditional views of truth, forming the basis of modern scientific thinking and summarised by Hicks:[7]

- Truth is outside of us - it does not depend on us
- Truth is discoverable - ask questions, investigate, form theories etc.
- Truth is authoritative - we do not control truth
- Truth can be communicated - we can learn truth from each other
- Truth is universal - the same the world over
- Truth is eternal

---

[5] Michael Green, *The Truth of God Incarnate* (London: Hodder & Stoughton, 1977), 9.

[6] Christopher Morgan, "Seventy C of E ministers admit they no longer believe in God," *Sunday Times* November 30, 1997.

[7] Hicks, *Truth: Could it Be True?*, 91-93.

We will thus proceed basing ourselves on such an understanding of truth, whereby certain non-negotiable truth kernels are taken as existing. Our task is to identify such kernels and relate them to the discussions between Islam and Christianity.

### How do we deal with conflicting truth claims?

Nevertheless, one needs to recognise from the outset that Truth claims can be relativised to some degree, depending on the subject.

On the subject of prayer, there is a common claim among Christians that Islam is legalistic and rule-bound, as evidenced by the five daily Islamic prayers containing virtually identical content. It is difficult to accept this as a statement of absolute truth. Some Muslim groups, such as Sufis, have developed devotional formats which seek communion with Allah, based on unstructured prayers. Similarly, some Christian groups prefer heavily liturgical worship; their prayers are no less structured than those of the standard Muslim prayer.

The creation story is largely similar between the Bible and Islamic scripture. There are minor points of difference, but they relate to peripheral matters and should not deflect us from a primary focus on the overall similarity of the two accounts.

Moreover, in certain of the prophetic accounts, such as the story of Joseph, the narrative detail is largely the same between the Bible and Islamic scripture. The differences in detail that do occur seem to be minor in terms of the overall structure, didactic function, and narrative thrust of the two accounts.

Thus the topics of prayer, the creation story, and some prophetic accounts demonstrate that wide-ranging subjects may allow for a degree of relativism in approach. Some even go so far as to say that there are various orthodoxies, and various truths on these topics.

### Perennial truths and the place of Jesus

But beyond areas such as these, there must be what Seyyed Hossein Nasr calls "perennial truths". He expresses this in terms of tradition, and it relates to the realm of the absolute. Nasr writes:

> "Tradition implies truths of a supraindividual character rooted in the nature of reality ... Tradition, like religion, is at once truth and presence ... It comes from the Source from which everything originates and to which everything returns ... Tradition is inextricably related to revelation and religion, to the

sacred, to the notion of orthodoxy, to authority, to the continuity and regularity of transmission of the truth ... the meaning of tradition has become related more than anything else to that perennial wisdom which lies at the heart of every religion."[8]

How are we to identify these "perennial truths"? It could be argued that this is the realm where we must vigorously oppose compromise or dilution. It is perhaps easier to identify such perennial truths in a secular context, for example, that murder for personal financial gain is wrong. But regarding perennial truths in the sphere of religious belief, postmodern society has made religious people much more cautious.

Cotterell[9] suggests that Truth claims should be divided into two categories: those which are verifiable as fact, and those which are verifiable only notionally. Cotterell provides the example of *Christ died for our sins* (1 Cor 15:3). The first part — *Christ died* — in principle is verifiable as fact. The second part is verifiable only notionally.

Cotterell's concept of "verifiable as fact" truth claims reconciles readily with Nasr's notion of perennial truths. But some fundamental tensions between Christianity and Islam exist in this area. In terms of the above example, there is a basic opposition between Christianity's account of Jesus' death on the cross and resurrection, versus Islam's rejection of the crucifixion, death and resurrection of Jesus at Q4:157-159.[10] As Netland points out:

> "... while it is logically possible for both [Christians and Muslims] to be wrong about the identity of Jesus ... both cannot be correct. At least one view of Jesus must be false."[11]

If all world religions depended on claims which were verifiable notionally, then a relativist approach would be much more appealing. But where claims verifiable as fact conflict between the religions, then a special challenge lies in trying to reach the Truth.

With regard to the second proposition in 1 Cor 15:3 — i.e. that Christ died *for our sins* — again this is at variance with Islamic dogma which

---

[8] Nasr, *Knowledge and the Sacred*, 68.

[9] Peter Cotterell, *Mission and Meaningless: The Good News in a World of Suffering and Disorder* (London: SPCK, 1990), 34.

[10] Ibid., 33.

[11] Harold A. Netland, *Dissonant Voices: Religious Pluralism and the Question of Truth* (Leicester: Apollos, 1991), 112.

holds that Jesus, like other prophets, was sent to show his community the Truth through transmitting Allah's word, and inform his community of the reward awaiting the righteous through following the Law and the punishment awaiting the ungodly through neglecting the Law. However, unlike the matter relating to Christ's death, we cannot assemble empirical evidence in support of either the Christian view or the Muslim view on this latter issue. Here it becomes rather an *experiential* matter (through the working of the Holy Spirit) or a matter of *faith* (declaring one's position without being able to assemble scientific evidence).

Thus an important quest should be the search for perennial truths, or those truths verifiable as fact. However, where the religions disagree on these perennial truths, a special challenge is posed which should not be ignored. As Cotterell comments: "It does no credit to scholarship to do other than admit to the fundamental and irreducible contradictions that exist among the myriad propositions of the world's religions."[12] Nasr would seem to agree, writing that:

> "Islam does not accept the idea of incarnation or filial relationship. In its perspective Jesus ... was a major prophet and spiritual pole of the whole Abrahamic tradition, but not a God-man or the son of God ... The Qur'an ... does not accept that he was crucified, but states that he was taken directly to heaven. This is the one irreducible 'fact' separating Christianity and Islam, a fact which is in reality placed there providentially to prevent a mingling of the two religions."[13]

Similarly, the prominent Muslim moderniser Mohamed Talbi (1921-2017) writes:

> "... in a dialogue, we need to give attention to making evident our differences for the purpose of being able to avoid illusions. To avoid the illusion that already tomorrow we will be able to move towards a more and more integrated unity. We practise different religious which, even though they converge on the upper level, are very different in the manner of choosing the paths towards it."[14]

---

[12] Cotterell, *Mission and Meaningless*, 35.

[13] Seyyed Hossein Nasr, *Islamic Life and Thought* (London: Allen & Unwin, 1981), 209.

[14] Mohamed Talbi, "Islamo–Christian Encounter Today: Some Principles," *MECC Perspectives* 4, no. 5 (July-August 1985): 9.

# Christian Approaches to Islam

> "Because of the replacement theology that Islam in general holds with regard to Christianity, it will often (although not always) be Christians who initiate the dialogue."[1]

## Is there a more helpful mindset to approaching Muslims than just "Conversion"?

"Conversion" is another of those terms that has acquired negative baggage in our postmodern times. In responding in the affirmative to the question, there is no suggestion that conversion is not legitimate as a goal of Christian engagement with Muslims. But a range of different mindsets are called for, according to the context. Christians and Muslims are extremely diverse, as we discussed earlier. If a key goal is for people to have fruitful and meaningful interactions, then vastly different styles of interaction need to be available.

That entails Christians entering a relationship with an open mind, allowing for the spontaneous and the unexpected, as is the case with normal human interaction.

It is important to avoid entering Christian-Muslim encounters with a template script driving the interaction.

## What are the objectives of inter-faith dialogue?

Many Christians and Muslims are seeking opportunities for dialogue, especially in Western countries where Muslim minorities have settled in increasing numbers since the Second World War. Why bother? This is a question many people ask from both religious communities. If dialogue participants are not convinced of the value of dialogue, then they will be ineffective dialogue partners.

Four principal objectives of dialogue between Christians and Muslims can be identified. The order of priority will differ according to the requirements and perspectives of the participants concerned.

1. *Mutual understanding.* Dialoguing about faith and cultural differences facilitates mutual understanding. Human history has witnessed many conflicts which have resulted from ignorance between communities. Many may have been avoided if there had

---

[1] Howarth, "9/11: A Call to Integrity in Mission," 5.

been a greater degree of mutual knowledge and understanding.

2. *Understanding God.* Dialogue should provide an opportunity for participants to advance in their knowledge of God and of his plan of salvation for all humanity. In this context, dialoguing on religious experience has a particular part to play.

3. *Witnessing.* Inter-faith dialogue should provide the participants with a forum to express their faith. Both Christianity and Islam consider speaking about one's beliefs and passing on these beliefs to others, or witnessing, as a significant and integral part of faith. As Roman Catholic Cardinal Francis Arinze comments, "for the Christian it is not only a right but a duty to share the faith."[2] Dialogue should take this fact into account and provide a forum for such witnessing to occur. Open and frank sharing of religious experience is important.

4. *Co-operation in relevant areas.* Dialogue should also provide some benefit to all parties involved. A fruitful dialogue between Christians and Muslims will provide the basis for joint activities for the advantage of all concerned. A particular case concerns humanitarian relief and development activities. Like Christianity, Islam teaches the importance of helping the poor and underprivileged, the orphaned and other disadvantaged groups. This shared concern should be explored to determine possible areas for co-operation.

Muslims and Christians might enter a dialogue with somewhat different objectives. Ataullah Siddiqui expresses Muslim motives in engaging in dialogue in the following terms: "Muslims have seen dialogue, in some respect, as a plea to explain their faith, but more than that they have viewed dialogue as an opportunity to face the growing challenge presented by atheism and materialism. Therefore, the theological dialogue for Muslims has received little attention."[3]

None of the above objectives needs entail compromising the central tenets of one's faith. This is a position on which Christians and Muslims can and do agree. As Douglas Pratt has perceptively observed, "the first and primary goal of dialogue is understanding,

---

[2] Arinze, *Religions for Peace*, 125.

[3] Ataullah Siddiqui, "The Presence of "Secular" in Christian–Muslim Relations: Reflections on the Da'wah, "Mission" and "Dialogue"," in *Christians and Muslims in the Commonwealth*, ed. Anthony O'Mahony and Ataullah Siddiqui (London: Altajir World of Islam Trust, 2001), 88.

not agreement."[4] The previously-mentioned Mohamed Talbi concurs with this view in writing on dialogue: "Never conceive of [dialogue] in terms of negotiation, in terms of concession, in terms of persuading the other. We only may conceive of it as a species of state of mind of somebody who tries to understand."[5]

In the above context, two questions posed during the 2003 series of the London Lectures are relevant:

- Do you agree with the Kandy statement[6] that "the result of dialogue is the work of the [Holy] Spirit?"

- How can Christians approach Christian-Muslim dialogue genuinely or sincerely when the ultimate hope is for Muslims to be won over to our side?

On the first, it should be noted that results of dialogue events are many and varied. A perusal of the many Christian-Muslim dialogue events organised by the World Council of Churches since 1970 suggests varying degrees of co-operation, or lack of it, flowing from the activities. The involvement of the Holy Spirit in such a process is very difficult to identify and quantify. What can be measured is the level and nature of human effort expended in dialogue, both during and after specific events. While the work of the Holy Spirit is important to consider, it is equally important that lack of success in inter-religious dialogue events should not be attributed solely to the Holy Spirit. Rather those involved should hold themselves accountable and creatively think of fresh new ways of undertaking the activity concerned.

On the second question, the above dialogue objectives provide for a central role for witnessing to one's faith, be it Christianity or Islam. Witnessing implies an eagerness on the part of a Christian or Muslim to share his/her faith in such a way that the other may choose to change faiths. This is perfectly legitimate, providing it is done on a level playing field. According to the 1977 WCC Guidelines on Dialogue, "Dialogue assumes the freedom of a person of any faith ...

---

[4] Douglas Pratt, "Christian–Muslim Encounter: From Diatribe to Dialogue," *Australian Religion Studies Review* 7, no. 1 (Autumn 1994): 13.

[5] Talbi, "Islamo–Christian Encounter Today," 10.

[6] "Dictionary of the Ecumenical Movement article on Interfaith Dialogue"

01 September 2002, https://www.oikoumene.org/en/resources/documents/wcc-programmes/interreligious-dialogue-and-cooperation/interreligious-trust-and-respect/ecumenical-dictionary-interfaith-dialogue.

to be convinced by the faith of another."[7] The unresolved issue here, of course, is the lack of freedom of Muslims to change their faith, as we have discussed.

## What are the best ways to do interfaith dialogue?

Interfaith dialogue comes in many forms. The best approach will depend on the gifts and interests of the people involved. The vast array of interfaith dialogue activities that have taken place across the world since the 1960s includes the following types:

- Dialogue among religious leaders, such as has taken place between the Grand Sheikh of Al-Azhar and both the Pope and the Archbishop of Canterbury.

- Dialogue among scholars, for which an excellent example is provided by the Building Bridges seminars (discussed below) that have taken place most years since 2002, involving Christian and Muslim scholars from many countries.

- Dialogue on religious experience, which offers the opportunity to move beyond political and social issues to discussion of perspectives on what it means to be experiencing the faiths in question. This often takes place in the form of interactions between local churches and mosques.

- Dialogue for conflict resolution, which relates specifically to politics and society, and which can be seen in meetings between Christians, Muslims and Jews to address long-standing conflicts.

- Dialogue on social concerns, where Christians and Muslims can meet to discuss common concerns about matters such as pornography in the media, anti-religious prejudice in education systems, religion and law, and so forth.

- Debates, where more contentious topics, be they matters of doctrine, politics and society, can be addressed in structured exchanges before large audiences.[8]

---

[7] "Guidelines on Dialogue with People of Living Faiths and Ideologies," 1 February 2010, accessed 22 September, 2010, http://www.oikoumene.org/en/resources/documents/wcc-programmes/interreligious-dialogue-and-cooperation/interreligious-trust-and-respect/guidelines-on-dialogue-with-people-of-living-faiths-and-ideologies.

[8] Some writers would not wish to include debate as a form of dialogue. However, it is a valuable member of the dialogue paradigm because it ensures that more difficult issues can be

## Are there any prerequisites for interfaith dialogue?

In order to achieve the above dialogue objectives, thought needs to be given to defining the rules of engagement. This issue has arisen regularly in Christian-Muslim interactions organised by the Church bodies. The value of agreed formats applies equally to dialogues on religious experience or social concerns as it does to discursive dialogue or Christian-Muslim debate.

Geffré argues for two essential conditions for dialogue to really take place.[9] First, in entering a dialogue, the otherness of the dialogue partner within the partner's cultural and religious identity should be respected. Both parties need to leave ingrained prejudices behind.

Second, each party needs to respect its own faith by speaking honestly and candidly about one's own faith perspective. As Michael Barnes observe, this loyalty to one's own faith position "is much more likely to get well-motivated liberal hackles rising."[10] Nevertheless, it is important not to enter a dialogue wearing a figurative mask, leaving behind essential elements of one's faith and only taking into the dialogue what is considered to be palatable to the dialogue partner; statements in dialogue do not necessarily have to win the approval and agreement of the dialogue partner. It is only if an unmasked face is shown that parties can serve as effective partners in the dialogue. In this context, Christians must ensure that any sense of guilt for colonialism which they might have does not translate to coyness or diffidence in their presentation of the Christian message in dialogue situations.

Swidler develops this further, presenting the ground rules to be followed by participants in dialogue.[11] The ideas of both Geffré and Swidler are consistent with the WCC's guidelines on dialogue mentioned above.

---

addressed rather than sidestepped. Many such debates are available on YouTube, involving leading Christian debaters who engage with Muslims such as Jay Smith, Bernie Power and Samuel Green.

[9] Claude Geffre, "Christian Uniqueness and Dialogue," *Focus* 2 (1993): 101-13. Cf. Anthony O'Mahony, "Christians and Muslim–Christian Relations: Theological Reflections," in *Christians and Muslims in the Commonwealth*, ed. Anthony O'Mahony and Ataullah Siddiqui (2001), 97.

[10] Michael Barnes, *Religions in Conversation* (London: SPCK, 1989), 4.

[11] Leonard Swidler, "Interreligious and Interideological Dialogue: The Matrix for All Systematic Reflection Today," in *Toward a Universal Theology of Religion*, ed. Leonard Swidler (Maryknoll, NY: Orbis, 1987), 14-16.

## Who should Christians be dialoguing with?

The headlong rush to promote Christian-Muslim dialogue and contact in Western countries since 9/11 has been of benefit to both Christians and Muslims in many ways. However, this process is having one particular negative spin-off. Other religious minorities are feeling somewhat sidelined in the process.

Hindus, Buddhists, Sikhs, and even Jews, are asking why Muslim minorities are receiving so much attention, and why so much emphasis now is on improved Christian-Muslim relations rather than on multi-faith harmony. Some are suggesting that the previous pattern of exclusion has merely been adjusted to accommodate Muslims in the inner circle, while others remain outside. Some even suggest that this is ironic, claiming that other minorities are more likely to work with the Western majority in a way which builds social cohesion, rather than seek to separate from it.

An illustration of this point occurred in a conversation I had with a Hindu lady who is involved in Hindu theological education and training with the youth of her community.[12] She explained that the young people she works with often express a sense of extreme frustration at what they observe to be preference in dialogue given to Muslims by Church leaders at the expense of other faiths. She said on one occasion, a group of Hindu youths she was speaking with asked: "What do we have to do in order to attract the same attention as Muslims. Do we have to hijack airliners and fly them into tall buildings in order to be noticed?" The lady concerned stressed that the question was in no way meant as an expression of intent; rather it reflected the increasing sense of exclusion felt by Hindus at what they consider to be favouritism accorded to Muslims in dialogue situations with Christians.

Nevertheless, leaders of the various churches often argue that the fragility of relations between Christians, Jews and Muslims means that they should be the primary partners in dialogue in the early 21$^{st}$ century, especially Muslims. This was the position taken by former Archbishop of Canterbury, George Carey, who launched the Archbishop's Initiative in Christian-Muslim Relations in 2002, which took precedence over a similar initiative towards Hindus,

---

[12] Personal communication, 26 March 2003.

Buddhists and others. Likewise, Catholic statements have been offered along similar lines:

> "... the event of the year 2000 will provide a great opportunity ... for interreligious dialogue... In this dialogue the Jews and the Muslims ought to have a pre-eminent place."[13]

A dialogue meeting of forty prominent Christians and Muslims was held in January 2002 at Lambeth Palace in London. The meeting was prompted by the shadows gathering over the Christian–Muslim relationship following the terrorist attacks of September 2001. At this first "Building Bridges" seminar, as the annual series came to be known, Bishop Kenneth Cragg pointed out that "there is much that is elitist about dialogue, and remote from the passions in the street."[14]

Here Bishop Cragg put his finger on one of the big challenges of dialogue activities, especially those undertaken by erudite scholars and prominent public figures. This problem can be compounded when certain groups are excluded from the dialogue. In the volume which emerged from the same seminar, Michael Ipgrave aptly states that "People and communities of other faiths hold many of the same concerns and values [as Christians and Muslims]; there is much scope for fruitful interaction on a wider inter faith basis."[15]

Herein lies a weakness of many dialogue activities; namely, that the massive surge in attention to Christian-Muslim dialogue is somehow pushing the Hindus, Buddhists, Jews, Sikhs and others to the margins of religious discourse in Western societies. In expanding the boundaries of the inner

> *The massive surge in attention to Christian-Muslim dialogue is somehow pushing the Hindus, Buddhists, Jews, Sikhs and others to the margins of religious discourse in Western societies.*

---

[13] Pope John Paul II, Apostolic letter on preparation for the jubilee year 2000, *Tertio Millennio Adveniente*, 10 November 1994, cited in *Interfaith Dialogue: The Teaching of the Catholic Church* (Committee for Other Faiths, Catholic Bishops' Conference of England and Wales, 2000), 25.

[14] Ipgrave, *The Road Ahead*, 15.

[15] Ibid., 120.

circle to accommodate Muslims, there is a risk that other faiths may feel shunned and relegated.

## Which Muslims should Christians be talking to?

In terms of specific Christian-Muslim relations, both Islam and Christianity are vast mosaics, made up of diverse elements of many shades and colours. Some Muslims and some Christians are getting on better than ever, and work closely together to build bridges between the two communities. However, there are also some Muslims and some Christians who figuratively draw the shutters on each other and are very suspicious of interfaith activity, seeing it as a sell-out of their faith.

In many ways, the important part of interfaith relations is not so much focusing on those who are already willing to cross lines, but rather in finding ways to involve those Muslims and Christians who refuse to do so. The situation won't be much helped if three groups emerge: one Christian refusing to work with Muslims, one Muslim refusing to work with Christians, and a third group of "professional dialoguers".

There should be engagement between all Christians and all Muslims, with the type of engagement determined by the nature of the groups involved. Clergy have a key role to play to ensure this happens at the grass roots level in local parishes.

## Why do Christians lack confidence and how can they best deal with it?

In order to build confidence, Christians should become more aware: study about the other faiths; learn more about their own faith so they feel confident in their knowledge of Christianity; and use their gifts appropriately to do what God has gifted them to do.

One reason for lack of confidence amongst Christians is a lack of knowledge about their own faith. Just as Christians should learn about other faiths, it is equally essential that Christians should learn more about their own faith, through distance learning programmes if they can't come to full time study at theological college, or through courses in churches such as Alpha courses and so forth. Before Christians take part in dialogue they need to be educated. They need to learn about the faith of those with whom they are dialoguing, but they also need to be very clear in their own minds why they are engaging in dialogue.

### Should Christians pray with people from other faiths?

Prayer with adherents of other faiths should be recommended, on condition that it is honest prayer. Christians should pray as they would normally pray, allowing the others to pray as they would normally pray. Christians should not pray in a way that they think might please the other but that is lacking in authenticity.

So, if Christians normally pray through Christ to God, then that is what they should be doing when praying in front of a Muslim, not doing it differently because a Muslim is present.

### How can Christians minister to Muslim women without causing family chaos?

This is a good question and shows appropriate sensitivity. Of course it will depend on the relationship between husband and wife, which can be as varied among Muslims as it is among Christians. It is crucial to understand the dynamics of the marriage relationship of the women you are encountering.

Some Muslim women will be open to discussing matters of faith and, indeed, may well exert an influence on their husbands. Other Muslim women will play a more subordinate role in the family and therefore may be very hesitant to have conversations about matters that their husbands did not approve.

It would be best to interact first with the Muslim women who evidently have no concerns about their husband's reaction, and to tread carefully and sensitively with those Muslim women who do have such worries. At the same time, if a Muslim woman asks you to explain your faith it would not be right not to do so in response to a request.

### Should Christians watch their language?

Choice of language can produce a negative reaction in certain circumstances. Consider the following report from a Christian periodical:

> "Leading Muslim organizations say it's time for Americans to stop using the phrase 'Judeo-Christian' when describing the values and character that define the United States. Better choices, they say, are 'Judeo-Christian-Islamic' or 'Abrahamic', referring to Abraham, the patriarch held in common by the monotheistic big three religions. The new language should be

used 'in all venues where we normally talk about Judeo-Christian values, starting with the media, academia, statements by politicians and comments made in churches, synagogues and other places,' said Agha Saeed, founder and chairman of the American Muslim Alliance, a political group headquartered in Fremont, Calif... Others take offense, arguing that to alter the phrase 'Judeo-Christian' is political correctness and revisionist history at its worst..."[16]

Interestingly, there has been some non-Muslim support for the suggestion:

"The movement to drop or change the phrase has some non-Muslim support, including the head of the National Council of Churches. The Rev. Bob Edgar, general secretary of the council, which represents 36 Christian denominations, said he prefers 'Abrahamic' to 'Judeo-Christian-Islamic' because it 'rolls off the tongue a little easier... The more inclusive we can be, the more committed we are to the founding fathers and mothers who struggled with the issue of respect for each other's religious faiths,' Edgar said."[17]

Such a suggestion is potentially highly emotive, as it can be considered to be challenging the very foundations of the identity of Western societies. Objections can be expressed in various ways. The above proposal could be taken to mean that Christians should watch their language in order not to offend Muslims by using phrases such as 'Judeo-Christian', but it is acceptable to offend some Christians and/or Westerners by using terms such as 'Judeo-Christian-Islamic' or 'Abrahamic'.

Furthermore, some Christians point out that in citizenship education for newly arriving immigrants, imparting a sense of belonging to the adopted nation involves identifying the values underpinning the society being adopted by the new arrivals, and this necessarily includes a recognition of the Judeo-Christian heritage of Western countries such as Britain, Australia and New Zealand.

It is hard to escape the impression that this discussion finds its context in a loss of confidence in much of the West regarding past history, and a willingness to reinterpret that past history in order to embrace minority viewpoints.

---

[16] Mark O'Keefe, "Has The United States Become Judeo-Christian-Islamic?," *Newhouse News Service,* 14 February, 2003, http://www.newhouse.com/archive/okeefe051503.html.
[17] Ibid.

Nevertheless, there is clearly a need to watch one's language in certain interfaith contexts. This particularly applies to references made to individual adherents of other faiths. Anti-vilification legislation is designed to protect people more than books, just as are laws relating to libel and slander. While it is legitimate to ask challenging questions of texts considered sacred by particular faiths, and even the doctrines arising from those texts, great care must be exercised in criticising publicly an individual or group of adherents of a particular faith.

A case which illustrates this point is a particular review on the Friends of Al-Aqsa website of a book[18] written by Baroness Caroline Cox and Dr John Marks.[19] The first part of the review focused on the book itself, challenging its interpretation of events in a range of ways. This is perfectly valid in terms of literary criticism. However, the second part of the review launched into a cutting critique of Baroness Cox's views and advocacy activities, quite apart from the book in focus. At this point the review itself lost a major part of its impact, and the reviewer would have been well advised to have watched his/her language in this regard.

**Watch your language**

---

[18] "Book Reviews," accessed 4 November, 2003, http://www.aqsa.org.uk/bookreviews/islamism.html.
[19] Caroline Cox and John Marks, *The 'West', Islam and Islamism* (London: Civitas, 2003).

## Do Christians have the right to ask critical questions about core Islamic beliefs?

This question serves as an umbrella for a myriad of more specific questions which are regularly articulated in non-Muslim discussion about Islam, such as the following questions posed at the 2003 series of the London Lectures:

- "In dialogue, what is an appropriate measure of challenging core aspects of Islam, such as (a) certain aspects of Muhammad's lifestyle (looting, numbers of wives, inconsistency etc.) and (b) the Qur'an, its inconsistencies and doctrines, all of which are ignored by many Muslims?"

- "Is there a place for polemics in Christian-Muslim dialogue?"

These questions raise the question of appropriate boundaries in Christian-Muslim relations. If such questions are posed in a clumsy fashion to Muslims, they could cause great offence and ill will and, as a result, a breakdown in communication. At the same time, the issue of sensitivity should surely not be the only factor involved in determining the dynamics of Christian-Muslim engagement. Freedom of speech, especially in a Western social context, should also be taken into account.

A particular case which led to legal action in Australia is relevant here. A Christian Pakistani migrant to Australia, Daniel Scot,[20] delivered a seminar on 9 March, 2002 to an audience of 250-300 in a church in Melbourne. The event was held by an organisation called Catch the Fire Ministry. In his address Scot discussed a range of topics: salvation in Islam; jihad in all its forms, especially holy war; deception in the Qur'an and Hadith; roles assigned to non-Muslims in the Qur'an and Hadith; women in Islam; and how to share the gospel with Muslims and answer their questions about Christianity.

The audience at the seminar included three white Australian converts to Islam, who were encouraged to attend the seminar by contacts within the Islamic Council of Victoria (ICV).[21] They lodged a complaint to the Victorian Equal Opportunity Commission (VEOC), in the context of the Victorian Racial and Religious Tolerance Act of

---

[20] Scot had fled from Pakistan when accused of blasphemy, a criminal offence under Pakistan legal codes.

[21] Piers Akerman, "When Legal Absurdity is Watched World-wide," *The Daily Telegraph* 4 March 2004.

January 2002. The VEOC then organised a conciliation meeting. The terms of conciliation were that Scott should apologise for what he had said and promise not to teach these subjects again in any form, oral or written. An extensive list was given of what he should apologise for.[22]

The conciliation meeting was unsuccessful, so it was then sent to Mediation as the next stage before the Victorian Civil and Administrative Tribunal (VCAT). In the Mediation stage, the Islamic Council of Victoria described Scot's teaching as inflammatory, and called for an apology and undertaking not to teach again in like manner. This Mediation stage was also unsuccessful. The case then went to a formal court hearing in October 2003. During the court hearing, Scot showed an encyclopaedic knowledge of the Islamic sacred texts, far more so than the three complainants.[23] Although the hearing found in favour of ICV, an appeal was lodged and the case was eventually dropped after out-of-court discussion and agreement.

The comments by Scot which triggered the formal complaint included, first, challenging questions about the Islamic sacred texts, and second, challenging questions about interpretation of the sacred texts by Muslim people. The case triggered a spate of articles in the Australian press, with writers arguing the case from various angles.

In a contribution to the debate, one Australian Muslim writer, Amir Butler, questioned the wisdom of the complainants in bringing the matters to the public attention via formal legal proceedings against Scot. He argued that the decision to appeal to anti-vilification legislation was the wrong reaction:

> *Amir Butler: "Political correctness has encouraged minorities to play the victim card, to vie for political influence by overstating and exaggerating being a victim."*

"... the only way to fight offensive ideas is to confront them intellectually. Legislation, punishments and smear campaigns cannot make bad ideas disappear. Instead, everyone must be allowed to express their views freely – good ideas will drive out bad. Political correctness has encouraged minorities to play the

---

[22] "Complaint no. A392/2002," Victorian Civil and Administrative Tribunal, 13 March, 2003).

[23] "When Legal Absurdity is Watched World-wide."

victim card, to vie for political influence by overstating and exaggerating being a victim. It's undignified, ineffective, and only serves to build resentment among the broader community that will quickly tire of being lectured as to how terribly racist it is – especially when that's untrue."[24]

Butler's identification of political correctness as an instrument in causing inter-faith friction resonates with discussion in this present study. He concluded his article with a forthright call for honest dialogue:

> "one can justifiably doubt a religion that can only exist within a fortress of anti-vilification laws and political correctness, a religion that cannot stand up to public scrutiny or criticism. A society based on this notion of political correctness is a society based on a foundation of lies – that all cultures, races, creeds and genders are the same and equal and that the state can, through legislation and ham-fisted social engineering, create cohesion among vastly different groups. The real key to social cohesion is honest dialogue. A dialogue, unfettered by political correctness, that is based on recognition that we have different ideas."[25]

The Scot case provides a good basis for answering questions about how forthright Christians should be in challenging core Islamic beliefs. Butler's comments also provide a very reasonable set of guidelines.

This case raises important issues relating to freedom of speech. There must be room in a society which values freedom of speech to ask hard questions of diverse sacred texts, be they Christian, Jewish, Islamic, Hindu or other. Indeed, such questioning is surely necessary in order to ensure that interpretation of those texts keeps pace with modern life, and is not frozen in time in a fundamentalist way.

At the same time, such questions should be posed in a way, and at a time, when reasoned discussion rather than offence is the more likely result. In other words, the issue is not so much what questions are being asked, but rather how they are being asked.

---

[24] Amir Butler, "Speak Up, I Won't Be Offended," *A True Word,* 11 July, 2003, http://www.atrueword.com/index.php/article/articleview/61/1/4.

[25] Ibid.

## What is the attitude of the Orthodox churches in relation to dialogue with Islam?

The Orthodox Christian churches have a long history of relationship with Islam. We will focus on the Russian and Greek churches, which represent two poles of world Orthodoxy.

The Russian Orthodox Church has been experiencing a significant revival since the fall of Communism. In the second decade of the 21$^{st}$ century, the church claimed around 150,000,000 adherents, making it the second largest Christian denomination after Roman Catholicism. In the years 2010-2016 a further 5,000 churches and 10,000 clergy were added, according to an August 2016 statement by Patriarch Kirill of Moscow and All Russia.[26]

The Church was not only active in meeting internal Christian needs. External relations with other faiths, including Islam, were receiving increasing attention, though Russian Orthodox activities in this regard were more directed to Muslim communities outside the country than to Russia's own fifteen million Muslim minority.[27]

For example, the year 2000 witnessed the holding of the Third Colloquium of the Joint Russian-Iranian Commission on 'Islam-Orthodoxy' Dialogue. It took place in Tehran from 24-25 January, 2000.[28] The participants in the Colloquium discussed the theme 'The Role of Interreligious Dialogue in International Relations'.

In 2007, when 138 Muslim scholars issued a call for Christian-Muslim dialogue entitled "A Common Word between Us and You", Patriarch Alexy II of Moscow and All Russia wrote a response in which he warmly welcomed the Muslim call for dialogue, and presented a carefully worded letter which achieved a delicate balance of praise and critique, stating:

> "The doctrinal dialogue between the Orthodox Church and Islam has considerably intensified recently. This happened not

---

[26] "The Russian Church increased for 5,000 churches and 10,000 clerics for the last six years," accessed 30 May, 2017, http://www.interfax-religion.com/?act=news&div=13150.

[27] Basil Cousins, "The Russian Orthodox Church, Tartar Christians and Islam," in *Eastern Christianity: Studies in Modern History, Religion and Politics*, ed. Anthony O'Mahony (London: Melisende, 2004), 339. Cf. also "Russian Orthodoxy: Contemporary Challenges in Society, Interreligious Encounters and Mission," in *World Christianity: Politics, Theology, Dialogues*, ed. Anthony O'Mahony and Michael Kirwan (London: Melisende, 2004), 308-46.

[28] "'Islam-Orthodoxy' Dialogue," accessed 3 November, 2003, http://www.russian-orthodox-church.org.ru/ne101251.htm.

only because we have to communicate more intensively and to build societal life together, but also because Christians and Muslims have come to face the same challenges which are impossible to meet on one's own. We have together encountered a pressure from the anti-religious worldview that claims universality and seeks to subject all the spheres of life in society. We are also witnesses to attempts to assert a 'new morality' that contradicts the moral norms supported by traditional religions. We should be together to face these challenges…

In many Muslim countries, Christians have enjoyed invariable support and have the freedom to live according to their own religious rules. But in some Islamic countries, the legislation prohibits the construction of churches, worship services and free Christian preaching. I hope that the letter of Islamic religious leaders and scholars proposing to intensify dialogue between our two religions will contribute to establishing better conditions for Christian minorities in such countries."[29]

The Greek Orthodox Church has interacted closely with the Islamic world for centuries, especially via steadily shrinking Orthodox communities in Muslim-majority Middle Eastern countries. Yannoulatos sees four phases in this engagement while Islam swept through the region. The first phase ($8^{th} - 9^{th}$ centuries) was characterised by Eastern Christians "taunting and undervaluing Islam". The second ($9^{th} - 14^{th}$ centuries) saw a flourishing of anti-Islamic polemical writings in the face of ongoing threats to Eastern Christendom. The third phase ($14^{th} - 15^{th}$ centuries) was characterised by "mild criticism and objective evaluation of Islam". With the fall of Constantinople to the Turks in 1453, Orthodox Christianity entered a fourth phase ($15^{th} - 18^{th}$ centuries), one of "silence and monologue".[30]

More recently Eastern Orthodoxy has been devoting its attention increasingly to a new phase of dialogue with Islam. This has coincided with changes in the Catholic Church following Vatican II, which Orthodoxy has observed, and developments within the World Council of Churches, in which Eastern Orthodoxy has participated.

---

[29] "Patriarch Alexy II of Moscow responds to Muslim theologians," accessed 30 May, 2017, http://antiochian.org/node/17594.

[30] Yannoulatos, "Byzantine and Contemporary Greek Orthodox Approaches to Islam'," 513-20.

The Greek Orthodox Patriarch Petros VII of Alexandria articulated in a 1998 speech his view of the origins and value of Orthodox-Muslim dialogue:

> "... dialogue between Christianity and Islam springs from the essence of Christianity, which is the foremost religion of dialogue... There are basic and essential differences between the religions of Christianity and Islam, which cannot be ignored... Subjects concerning man and the world, especially matters which deal with everyday problems, can lead in this dialogue... Communication and co-operation between religions make an essential contribution to the abolition of religious fanaticism, an intellectual sickness of the religious person... Productive dialogue can help realise heavenly peace on Earth, and protect the holiness of life and man's dignity... Dialogue which is based, not only on theological matters, but on worldly issues, can be both hopeful and fruitful..."[31]

However, in the same speech, Petros VII reflected the historical concerns of Eastern Orthodox Christians in Arab lands in alluding to issues of religious freedom:

> "Orthodoxy coexists and seeks dialogue with Islam; dialogue which presupposes freedom of speech and equality between the two parties... In Eastern Christianity one sees respect towards the religious experience of others, forbearance and mutual understanding... For centuries, a large part of Orthodoxy lived in the Islamic world, although not always as an equal member of its society... dialogue is necessary, and indeed, is the only acceptable way to bring our two religions closer... Dialogue is necessary if we are to overcome the past and the present of alienation, confrontation, enmity and hatred."[32]

In certain circumstances the Orthodox church interaction with Muslims has been coloured by factors falling outside areas of Church authority. A case in point is found in Bulgaria, where the Communist government forced the Turkish and other Muslim minority groups[33] to adopt non-Muslim names in 1985. This caused an outcry among Bulgarian Muslims at the time, but the Bulgarian Orthodox Church authorities remained largely silent on the issue, in contrast with the active role the Bulgarian Church had played in saving Bulgarian Jews

---

[31] Greek Orthodox Patriarch Petros VII of Alexandria, "Christianity and Islam in Dialogue. Address of His Beatitude to the 12th International Meeting "People and Religion"," 31 August, 1998, accessed 3 November, 2003, http://www.greece.org/gopatalex/islam.html.

[32] Ibid.

[33] The Muslim minority represents 10-15% of Bulgaria's total population of around 8 million.

from deportation to Nazi camps during World War Two. This silence contributed to an atmosphere of mistrust and bitterness between Bulgarian Muslims and the Orthodox church.

## How should Christians and Muslims report past history?

In a volume published from the first Building Bridges seminar, a series of annual Christian-Muslim dialogues among scholars, Michael Ipgrave writes as follows:

> *The task of the historian is essentially to report and interpret past events, not deliberately report some of them in more detail in order to facilitate present-day ideological whims and preferences.*

"... while the past cannot be altered, the way in which it is remembered is not beyond our control. By their choice of key episodes on which to focus, and by their interpretations of those episodes, historians can significantly influence perceptions and attitudes in the present, and so help to shape the future."[34]

Ipgrave's approach seems to be embraced in David Kerr's thumbnail sketch of past Christian-Muslim history in the same volume.[35] He mentions what he sees as the two eras of European imperialism: the Crusades and the imperial expansion of the 16$^{th}$-19$^{th}$ centuries. No mention is made of the Ottoman conquest of Constantinople in 1453, Turkish imperial expansion into the Balkans and Central European states, or the massacres of the Armenians by the Ottoman Turks during the First World War.

Questions should be asked about this approach to history writing. The task of the historian is essentially to report and interpret past events,[36] not deliberately report some of them in more detail in order to facilitate present-day ideological whims and preferences. If the latter becomes the case, subsequent generations are likely to conclude that history gave way to propaganda and indoctrination in the name of better interfaith relations.

---

[34] Ipgrave, *The Road Ahead*, 25.

[35] David A. Kerr, "Christian–Muslim Relations: Lessons from History," in *The Road Ahead: A Christian–Muslim Dialogue*, ed. Michael Ipgrave (London: Church House Publishing, 2002), 26-37.

[36] Of course, historians face great challenges in pursuing these goals, and they never do nor can report and interpret the totality of past events. Cf. Karl Popper, *The Open Society and its Enemies*, vol. 2, ch.13.

It is true that no school or university course in history can cover all areas of the field, and a large measure of selection is required. The decision then should become how this selection can be carried out in a way that does not merely feed one particular ideological approach, but rather respects scholarly integrity and reflects a suitable diversity of viewpoints.

# Further Questions

In this small book we set out to address questions that were posed during many public lectures on Islam and Christian-Muslim Relations given in churches and other venues in a twenty-year from 1996.

The questions included do not reflect all questions asked in those events, nor do they represent all questions that could be asked. Rather they provide a representative sample, and hopefully the answers recorded here are of use to readers.

It would be helpful to conclude our volume with a list of further questions that have arisen in different contexts or on different topics. We present below a set of questions on topics connected with Theology and Evangelism which have not been addressed in earlier discussion in this book but which receive detailed attention in other books.[37] Also included are a set of questions addressed by Christians to Muslims during visits to mosques.

## Questions about Theology and Evangelism

- What does the Quran say about Jesus? How does this differ with the biblical Jesus?

- How can we use what they already know about Jesus as a starting point to talk about him further?

- We hear stories of Jesus revealing himself to Muslims in dreams and visions. Should we encourage our Muslim friends to be open to this or even seeking it, or should we point them to the Bible first?

- What aspects of Christianity should we emphasise when sharing with Muslims? E.g. Emphasis on love and the Father heart of God to address the orphan spirit by making us His children?

---

[37] Cf. Badru D. Kateregga and David W. Shenk, *Islam and Christianity: a Muslim and a Christian in dialogue* (Grand Rapids: Eerdmans, 1980); Gerhard Nehls, *Christians Ask Muslims* (Belville: SIM International / Life Challenge, 1987); Bernie Power, *Understanding Jesus and Muhammad* (Australia: Acorn Press, 2016), and a number of other works.

- How does Islam see the possibility and pathway to intimacy with God? How does that differ with Christianity? Especially in view of Jer 31:3 and Jn 3:16-17.

- "Does Islam in its Texts have similar commandments as our Christian great commandment to love God and love your neighbour?"

- "Are we all irrespective of faith praying to the one God?"

- "Muslims have often said that they serve same God as Christians. How do we help them understand they do not, but also understand their perspective?"

- How does a context of an honour- shame culture affect the way we present the gospel to Muslims?

## Questions to ask Muslims when visiting a mosque

- Muhammad
    - What was Muhammad's religion before he began receiving his revelations at the age of 40?
    - With the 200-year gap between the death of Muhammad and the earliest biographies, how sure can we be about the historical record of Muhammad?
    - The Sira says that Muhammad contemplated suicide. Why was that?
    - What makes Muhammad the best and last prophet other than having unified the Arabs?
    - Why did Muhammad reject Christianity?
    - Do some Muslims elevate Muhammad in a way that is inappropriate?
    - What are the significant differences between the Prophet in Mecca and the Prophet in Medina? (And is it relevant for da'wa?)

- Qur'an and Hadith
    - Was the Qur'an already written in Heaven and to what extent does it reflect the circumstances in Muhammad's life?
    - How important is a chronology of the Qur'anic surahs?
    - If the Qur'an is perfect, why do Muslims need the Hadith, Sunnah, Sira, etc?
    - Are we as Christians allowed to hold and read the Qur'an?
    - How accurate are the translations of the Qur'an, given that the Qur'an is seen as God's word and therefore it is only accurate in Arabic?
    - The Qur'an was not written during the life of Muhammad. How much can you rely on oral accounts?
    - Does the Quran say anything about how to live as a Muslim and be a good citizen under foreign rule?
    - Do the Hadith collections apply equally in the 21st century?
    - Are the Hadith collections all equally valid and if not how would one know?
- History
    - Did Islam expand by the sword or by peaceful means?
    - How would you explain the great success of the initial Islamic expansion, but that it was defeated in 732 by Charles Martel?
    - When did problems between Christians and Muslims begin?
    - Why is Spain portrayed in such utopian terms under Moorish rule?
    - Did any religious minorities suffer any discrimination in Islamic Spain?
    - What were the causes of the Crusades?

- o What was the process that caused some territories like Turkey to go from being largely Christian to Muslim?
- Islam and today's world
  - o Is Islam the best faith for the 21st century? Why?
  - o How Islamic is ISIS? What about some of the things they have done, for instance destroying churches?
  - o Do men and women interact during prayers? Why do they separate men and women during worship?
  - o Is there an instruction that a Muslim can only vote for a Muslim as some Indonesian Muslims claimed during the elections for the Mayor of Jakarta in early 2017?
  - o Is the Constitution of Medina relevant for today's world?
  - o Is inter-marriage allowed? Can a non-Muslim man marry a Muslim woman without converting?
- Islamic Theology and practice
  - o Do Muslim people have free will?
  - o How does a fast work? Are you able to use a tooth pick?
  - o Why do Muslims pray towards Mecca?
- Islamic Diversity
  - o Are there Sufis at this mosque? Is there a space where they can express themselves?
  - o Do you have other Muslim groups that come to your mosque, for instance Shias?
- Islamic Views of Christians and Christianity
  - o What do you believe regarding the Trinity?
  - o What do you believe regarding the Jesus of Christianity?
- Imams
  - o Where are Imams trained, and are there plans to train them locally?

- If an imam is needed would a woman be considered. Are there female imams?
- Just as Christians can study Islam in seminaries, is Christianity taught in Muslim religious schools?
- Do you personally wish to see the Caliphate re-established?

## Bibliography

Akerman, Piers. "When Legal Absurdity is Watched World-wide." *The Daily Telegraph*, 4 March 2004.

Al-Bukhari, Muhammed ibn Ismaiel. *Sahih al-Bukhari: the translation of the meanings of Sahih al-Bukhari: Arabic-English*. Translated by Muhammad Muhsin Khan. 9 vols. Vol. 9, Riyadh: Darussalam, 1997.

Al-Qayrawani, 'Abdullah Ibn Abi Zayd. "The Risala: A Treatise on Maliki Fiqh." accessed 16 May, 2017, http://www.iiu.edu.my/deed/lawbase/risalah_maliki/.

Al-Turabi, Hassan Abdullah. "Opinion on Apostasy stirs a Heated Debate in Islamic Juristic Circles." *The Diplomat*, no. 2 (Muharram 1417 / June 1996).

Alam, M. Shahid. "Pakistan 'Recognizes' Israel." accessed 7 September, 2003, http://www.khilafah.com/home/category.php?DocumentID=8225&TagID=2.

Ali, Abdullah Yusuf. *The Meaning of the Holy Qur'an*. New ed. Beltsville, Maryland: Amana Publications, 1989.

Amnesty International. "Pakistan: Use and Abuse of the Blasphemy Laws." July 1994, https://www.amnesty.org/en/documents/asa33/008/1994/en/.

Arab West Report. "A Statement by the Muslim Scholars in Europe." 23 October, 2001, accessed 10 July, 2017, http://www.arabwestreport.info/en/year-2001/week-43/18-statement-muslim-scholars-europe.

Arie, Sophie. "Muslim Wins Italian Court Ban on Crucifixes in Classroom." *The Guardian*, 27 October, 2003.

Arinze, Francis. *Religions for Peace: A Call for Solidarity to the Religions of the World* London: Darton, Longman & Todd, 2002.

Bakhsh, Madeeha. "Trial of blasphemy accused Asia Bibi 'likely' to resume in June." April 21, 2017, accessed 29 July, 2017, https://www.christiansinpakistan.com/trial-of-blasphemy-accused-asia-bibi-likely-to-resume-in-june/.

Barnes, Michael. *Religions in Conversation*. London: SPCK, 1989.

"BBC Religion & Ethics." accessed 17 May, 2017, http://www.bbc.co.uk/religion.

Bennett, Clinton. *In Search of Muhammad*. London & New York: Cassell, 1998.

Birt, Yahya. "Lies! Damn Lies! Statistics and Conversions." *Q-News*, no. 350 (October 2003).
"Book Reviews." accessed 4 November, 2003, http://www.aqsa.org.uk/bookreviews/islamism.html.
Bowker, Sam. "The Australian Mosque." accessed 17 May, 2017, http://www.abc.net.au/news/2016-09-23/the-australian-mosque/7868256.
Brierley, Peter. "Muslim Growth in the United Kingdom and Worldwide." accessed 17 May, 2017, https://www.lausanneworldpulse.com/research-php/654/03-2007.
Butler, Amir. "Speak Up, I Won't Be Offended." *A True Word*, 11 July, 2003. http://www.atrueword.com/index.php/article/articleview/61/1/4.
Center, Pew Research. "The World's Muslims: Religion, Politics and Society." 2013, accessed 16 May, 2017, http://www.pewforum.org/2013/04/30/the-worlds-muslims-religion-politics-society-overview/.
Chapman, Colin. "Going Soft on Islam?". *Vox Evangelica* XIX (1989): 7-31.
"The Church of England: Resurrection?". *The Economist,* January 9, 2016. http://www.economist.com/news/britain/21685473-parts-established-church-are-learning-their-immigrant-brethren-resurrection.
"Complaint no. A392/2002." Victorian Civil and Administrative Tribunal, 13 March, 2003.
Cotterell, Peter. *Mission and Meaningless: The Good News in a World of Suffering and Disorder* London: SPCK, 1990.
Cousins, Basil. "The Russian Orthodox Church, Tartar Christians and Islam." In *Eastern Christianity: Studies in Modern History, Religion and Politics*, edited by Anthony O'Mahony, 338-71. London: Melisende, 2004.
———. "Russian Orthodoxy: Contemporary Challenges in Society, Interreligious Encounters and Mission." In *World Christianity: Politics, Theology, Dialogues*, edited by Anthony O'Mahony and Michael Kirwan, 308-46. London: Melisende, 2004.
Cox, Caroline, and John Marks. *The 'West', Islam and Islamism* London: Civitas, 2003.
Cragg, Kenneth. *The Call of the Minaret*. Oxford: Oxford University Press, 1956.

Dardashti, Michelle. "Survey: Saudi Arabian Textbooks Filled with Hatred of West, Jews'." accessed 10 April, 2004, http://www.jta.org/page_view_story.asp?intarticleid=12426&intcategoryid=3.

"EU embarrassed as poll labels Israel world's biggest threat." 3 November, 2003, accessed 20 December, 2003, http://story.news.yahoo.com/news?tmpl=story&u=/afp/20031103/wl_mideast_afp/eu_poll_israel_031103172948.

"The ex-Muslim Britons who are persecuted for being atheists." accessed 16 May, 2017, http://www.bbc.com/news/magazine-34357047.

Fraser, Giles. "Evangelicals Have Become This Century's Witch Burners." *The Guardian*, 14 July, 2003.

Funk, Marco, and Roderick Parkes. "Refugees versus terrorists."Issue Alert no. 6: European Union Institute for Security Studies, January 2016, http://www.iss.europa.eu/uploads/media/Alert_6_Refugees_versus_terrorists.pdf.

Garavelli, Dani. "The Attraction of the Veil." *The Times*, 10 March, 2002.

Garlow, James L. *A Christian's response to Islam*. Eastbourne, UK: Kingsway, 2005.

Geffre, Claude. "Christian Uniqueness and Dialogue." *Focus* 2 (1993): 101-13.

"Germany approves huge mosque construction." accessed 17 May, 2017, http://www.middle-east-online.com/english/?id=27616.

Gerwehr, Scott, and Sara Daly. "Al-Qaida: Terrorist Selection and Recruitment." In *The McGraw-Hill Homeland Security Handbook: The Definitive Guide for Law Enforcement, EMT, and all other Security Professionals*, 73-89. New York: McGraw-Hill, 2005.

Greek Orthodox Patriarch Petros VII of Alexandria. "Christianity and Islam in Dialogue. Address of His Beatitude to the 12th International Meeting "People and Religion"." 31 August, 1998, accessed 3 November, 2003, http://www.greece.org/gopatalex/islam.html.

Green, Michael. *The Truth of God Incarnate*. London: Hodder & Stoughton, 1977.

"Guidelines on Dialogue with People of Living Faiths and Ideologies." 1 February 2010, accessed 22 September, 2010, http://www.oikoumene.org/en/resources/documents/wcc

-programmes/interreligious-dialogue-and-cooperation/interreligious-trust-and-respect/guidelines-on-dialogue-with-people-of-living-faiths-and-ideologies.

Harris, Myles. *Tomorrow is Another Country*. London: Civitas, 2003.

Hicks, Peter. *Truth: Could it Be True?* Carlisle: Solway, 1996.

Hillenbrand, Carole. *The Crusades: Islamic Perspectives* New York: Routledge, 2000.

Hitchens, Peter. "Will Britain Convert to Islam?" *The Mail on Sunday,* 2 November, 2003. http://www.femail.com/pages/standard/article.html?in_page_id=2&in_article_id=201325.

Hoque, Aminul. "Young British Muslims alienated by 'us versus them' rhetoric of counter-terrorism." *The Conversation,* September 29, 2017. http://theconversation.com/young-british-muslims-alienated-by-us-versus-them-rhetoric-of-counter-terrorism-46117.

Howarth, Toby. "9/11: A Call to Integrity in Mission." CMS Annual Sermon 2002. London: Church Missionary Society, 2002.

Huntington, Samuel P. "The Clash of Civilizations?," *Foreign Affairs*, no. 72 (Summer 1993):22-49.

Huntington, Samuel P. *The Clash of Civilizations and the Remaking of World Order*. New York: Simon & Schuster, 1996.

Ibn Abi Zayd al-Qayrawani, 'Abd Allah ibn 'Abd al-Rahman. *Al-Risala*. London: Ta-Ha, 1999.

*Interfaith Dialogue: The Teaching of the Catholic Church* Committee for Other Faiths, Catholic Bishops' Conference of England and Wales, 2000.

Ipgrave, Michael . *The Road Ahead: A Christian–Muslim Dialogue*. London: Church House Publishing, 2002.

"Islam and the Textbooks." accessed 30 May, 2017, http://www.meforum.org/559/islam-and-the-textbooks.

"'Islam-Orthodoxy' Dialogue." accessed 3 November, 2003, http://www.russian-orthodox-church.org.ru/ne101251.htm.

Kateregga, Badru D., and David W. Shenk. *Islam and Christianity: a Muslim and a Christian in dialogue*. Grand Rapids: Eerdmans, 1980.

Kaye, Bruce. "Many Aspects of Pluralism." *St Mark's Review*, no. 171 (Spring 1997): 2-5.

Kerr, David A. "Christian–Muslim Relations: Lessons from History." In *The Road Ahead: A Christian–Muslim Dialogue,* edited by Michael Ipgrave, 26-37. London: Church House Publishing, 2002.

Laffan, Michael. *The makings of Indonesian Islam: orientalism and the narration of a Sufi past*. Princeton, N.J.: Princeton University Press, 2011.

"List of mosques in the United States." accessed 17 May, 2017, https://en.wikipedia.org/wiki/List_of_mosques_in_the_United_States.

Maghniyyah, M.J. *The Five Schools of Islamic Law: Al-Hanafi, al-Hanbali, al-Ja'fari, al-Maliki, al-Shafi'i*. Qum, Iran: Ansariyan, 1995.

Middleton, J. R., and B. J. Walsh. *Truth is Stranger than it Used to Be: Biblical Faith in a Postmodern Age*. London: SPCK, 1995.

Mirahmadi, Hedieh. "Jihadi Tomb Raiders." *National Review*, December 13, 2002. http://old.nationalreview.com/comment/comment-mirahmadi121302.asp.

Mohammed, Ovey N. *Muslim-Christian Relations: Past, Present, Future*. Maryknoll: Orbis Books, 1999.

Morgan, Christopher. "Seventy C of E ministers admit they no longer believe in God." *Sunday Times*, November 30, 1997.

"Mosques and Islamic Schools in New Zealand." accessed 18 May, 2017, https://www.salatomatic.com/reg/New-Zealand/uJt2QgpcxO.

"Muslims have the right to attack America." 11 November, 2001, accessed 15 May, 2017, https://www.theguardian.com/world/2001/nov/11/terrorism.afghanistan1.

Nasr, Seyyed Hossein. *Islamic Life and Thought*. London: Allen & Unwin, 1981.

———. *Knowledge and the Sacred*. New York: Crossroad, 1981.

"'Negotiate with Bin Laden': Mowlam." *Guardian*, April 8, 2004.

Nehls, Gerhard. *Christians Ask Muslims*. Belville: SIM International / Life Challenge, 1987.

Netland, Harold A. *Dissonant Voices: Religious Pluralism and the Question of Truth*. Leicester: Apollos, 1991.

Netto, Anil. "Malaysia: PAS Winning Few Hearts so Far." *Asia Times Online*, March 6, 2004. http://www.atimes.com/atimes/Southeast_Asia/FC06Ae04.html.

O'Brien, Mike. "The Threat of the Modern Kharijites." Paper presented at the conference 'Militant Islam in Asia: The

Challenges', Royal United Service Institute for Defence Studies: London, 21 November 2002.

O'Keefe, Mark. "Has The United States Become Judeo-Christian-Islamic?" *Newhouse News Service,* 14 February, 2003. http://www.newhouse.com/archive/okeefe051503.html.

O'Mahony, Anthony. "Christians and Muslim–Christian Relations: Theological Reflections." In *Christians and Muslims in the Commonwealth,* edited by Anthony O'Mahony and Ataullah Siddiqui, 90-128, 2001.

Ohana, David. "Are Israelis the New Crusaders?" *The Palestine-Israel Journal,* 13, no. 3, 2006. http://www.pij.org/details.php?id=865.

Olayemi, Abdul Azeez Maruf, Alabi, Abdul Majeed Hamzah & Buang, Ahmad Hidayah. "Islamic Human Rights Law: A Critical Evaluation of UIDHR & CDHRI in Context of UDHR", *Journal of Islam, Law and Judiciary,* no. 1 (2015): 27-36.

"Open letter to Dr. Ibrahm Awwad Al-Badri, alias 'Abu Bakr Al-Baghdadi' and to the fighters and followers of the self-declared 'Islamic state'." 24th Dhul-Qi'da 1435 AH/19th September 2014 CE, accessed 13 May, 2017, http://www.lettertobaghdadi.com.

"Patriarch Alexy II of Moscow responds to Muslim theologians." accessed 30 May, 2017, http://antiochian.org/node/17594.

Pawson, David. *The Challenge of Islam to Christians.* London: Hodder & Stoughton, 2003.

Petre, Jonathan. "Carey's Scathing Assault on Islam." 27 March, 2004, accessed 10 June, 2005, http://smh.com.au.

Pires, Tome. *The Suma Oriental of Tome Pires.* London: The Hakluyt Society, 1944.

Polisar, D. "Do Palestinians Want a Two-State Solution?" *Mosaic,* April 3, 2017. https://mosaicmagazine.com/essay/2017/04/do-palestinians-want-a-two-state-solution/.

Popper, Karl. *The Open Society and its Enemies.* Vol. 2 The High Tide of Prophecy: Hegel, Max and the Aftermath, London: Routledge & Kegan Paul, 1962.

Power, Bernie. *Understanding Jesus and Muhammad.* Australia: Acorn Press, 2016.

Pratt, Douglas. "Christian–Muslim Encounter: From Diatribe to Dialogue." *Australian Religion Studies Review* 7, no. 1 (Autumn 1994).

"Press Release." 7 November, 2001, accessed 7 September, 2003, http://www.almuhajiroun.com.

Ramachandra, Vinoth. *Faiths in Conflict?: Christian Integrity in a Multicultural World*. USA: IVP Academic, 2000.

"Real life: Australian woman Lydia on why she converted to Islam." accessed 19 May, 2017, http://www.news.com.au/lifestyle/real-life/real-life-australian-woman-lydia-on-why-she-converted-to-islam/news-story/560bf829839cffc6b5ea6085f4a5e672.

*Reciprocity and Beyond: A Muslim Response to the European Churches' Document on Islam*. Leicester: Islamic Foundation, 1997.

"Remarks by the President at Islamic Society of Baltimore." The White House, Office of the Press Secretary, February 03, 2016, accessed 22 May, 2017, https://obamawhitehouse.archives.gov/the-press-office/2016/02/03/remarks-president-islamic-society-baltimore.

Ricklefs, Merle. *The Seen and Unseen Worlds in Java, 1726-1749: History, Literature, and Islam in the Court of Pakubuwana II*. St. Leonards, N.S.W.: Asian Studies Association of Australia, 1998.

Riddell, Peter G. "Britain Pays the Price for Complacency." *American Spectator,* June 6, 2017. https://spectator.org/britain-pays-the-price-for-complacency/.

———. *Christians and Muslims: Pressures and potential in a post-9/11 world*. Leicester: Inter-Varsity Press, 2004.

Riddell, Peter G., and Peter Cotterell. *Islam in Context: Past, Present and Future*. Grand Rapids: Baker Academic, 2003.

"Rural Australia attracting immigrants." accessed 17 May, 2017, http://www.workpermit.com/news/rural-australia-attracting-immigrants-20060130.

"The Russian Church increased for 5,000 churches and 10,000 clerics for the last six years." accessed 30 May, 2017, http://www.interfax-religion.com/?act=news&div=13150.

Saeed, Abdullah. *Freedom of Religion, Apostasy and Islam*. London: Routledge, 2004.

Serhan, Yasmeen. "France's Disappearing Mosques." accessed 17 May, 2017, https://www.theatlantic.com/news/archive/2016/08/french-mosques-islam/493919/.

Sewall, Gilbert. *Islam in the Classroom: What the Textbooks Tell Us.* New York: American Textbook Council, 2008.

Siddiqui, Ataullah. "Issues in Co-existence and Dialogue: Muslims and Christians in Britain." In *Muslim–Christian Perceptions of Dialogue Today: Experiences and Expectations*, edited by Jacques Waardenburg. Leuven: Peeters, 2000.

———. "The Presence of "Secular" in Christian–Muslim Relations: Reflections on the Da'wah, "Mission" and "Dialogue"." In *Christians and Muslims in the Commonwealth*, edited by Anthony O'Mahony and Ataullah Siddiqui, 67-89. London: Altajir World of Islam Trust, 2001.

Sloane-White, Patricia. *Corporate Islam: Sharia and the modern workplace*, New York: Cambridge University Press, 2017.

Solomon, S. and Wakeling, K. *A Comparison Table of Shari'ah Law and English Law*, London: Christian Concern for our Nation, 2009.

Steenbrink, Karel. *Dutch Colonialism and Indonesian Islam: Contacts and Conflicts 1596-1950.* Amsterdam: Rodopi, 2006.

"Storm over Italy crucifix ruling." 26 October, 2003, accessed 29 July, 2017, http://news.bbc.co.uk/1/hi/world/europe/3215445.stm.

Swidler, Leonard. "Interreligious and Interideological Dialogue: The Matrix for All Systematic Reflection Today." In *Toward a Universal Theology of Religion*, edited by Leonard Swidler. Maryknoll, NY: Orbis, 1987.

Talbi, Mohamed. "Islamo–Christian Encounter Today: Some Principles." *MECC Perspectives* 4, no. 5 (July-August 1985).

"Theodor Nöldeke." accessed 2 June, 2017, https://en.wikipedia.org/wiki/Theodor_N%C3%B6ldeke - N.C3.B6ldeke_Chronology.

"Transcript of Osama bin Laden videotape." December 13, 2001, accessed 2 June, 2015, http://www.cnn.com/2001/US/12/13/tape.transcript.

"Two Sides of a Different Coin? Anthony McRoy talks to Sheikh Omar Bakri Muhammad and Shagufta Yaqub." *Third Way*, March 2003, 21.

"UN Security Council Resolution 1373." 2001, accessed 30 April, 2003, http://www.un.org/News/Press/docs/2001/sc7158.doc.htm.

"Universal Declaration of Human Rights." accessed 16 May, 2017, http://www.un.org/en/universal-declaration-human-rights/.

"US is the greatest threat to world peace: poll." *New York Post,* January 5, 2014. http://nypost.com/2014/01/05/us-is-the-greatest-threat-to-world-peace-poll/.

"Why Not All Muslims Support the Radicals." *Church Times*, 3 January, 2003.

Yannoulatos, Anastasios. "Byzantine and Contemporary Greek Orthodox Approaches to Islam'." *Journal of Ecumenical Studies* 33, no. 4 (Fall 1996): 512-27.

Zebiri, Kate. *Muslims and Christians Face to Face*. Oxford: Oneworld Publications, 1997.

www.ingramcontent.com/pod-product-compliance
Lightning Source LLC
Chambersburg PA
CBHW050600300426
44112CB00013B/2004